What Are We Doing?!

Radical Self-Care for the Hustle Culture

Joelle Connors Moray, M.S., NCC

ISBN: 978-1-955750-96-7

Table of Contents

For Dad.

Thank you for giving me my sense of humor, my obsession with curiosity, an understanding of passive voice, and the love of the Oxford Comma.

I hope this book makes you proud.

Introduction

No One Should Be Dying This Way

To anyone who has ever felt like they are running on a treadmill of their own ambition, to those who lie awake at night with racing thoughts of to-do lists and existentialism, this book is for you. Together, we'll explore what it means to live intentionally in a world that tells us we must always do more, be more, and have more.

As you delve into the following pages, you will uncover the myths that fuel what has been and still is frequently referred to as "the hustle culture." We'll examine the toll this hustle culture takes on our well-being, and discover, instead, how to cultivate a life of purpose, joy, and harmony. From setting boundaries to embracing mindfulness, I'll share with you how to redefine success and build communities of compassion and intentionality.

This book is a roadmap for anyone who feels overwhelmed by the demands of modern life and seeks a more fulfilling path. This book also provides an easy-to-understand protocol that includes radical curiosity, taking inspired action, adaptability, resilience, resourcing, and something I created called the Press Pause Method. Pressing pause teaches us how slowing down dramatically increases productivity and exponentially increases success in all areas of life.

The Press Pause Method is evidence-based and has been proven to decrease stress, anxiety, ADHD, and more, while improving sleep, focus, and memory. Finally, I'll conclude with a call to build community around slowing down to get ahead. This is way beyond success, relationships, communication, and self-care. It's a rallying cry for a trailblazing, global movement of longevity.

Mom's Story

"Something is wrong with Mom. She seems off." This was a conversation I had with my brothers sometime around 2009. Mom was always gregarious, fun, quirky, and slightly eccentric, which is why her seeming "off" might have been rather normal for her.

However, only a few months later came a diagnosis – Dementia. This was quite an unexpected blow to everyone. Cognitive decline does not run in our family. Quite the opposite; most people on that side of our family lived a long time with full mental faculties.

My great-grandmother lived to almost 99, my grandfather to the age of 87, and as I write this, I have two great uncles who are 85 and 86, both of whom are healthy—at least cognitively. So, if genetics aren't a factor, what else could have been causing this?

My mom never lost her memory—a hallmark of what is commonly thought of as a sign of Dementia and Alzheimer's. She lost her ability to speak, or word-finding, a condition known as Primary Progressive Aphasia. When you look at my mom's life as a whole, it's clear to me and my family what her real issue was – environmental, emotional, and mental stressors.

Complex trauma refers to exposure to multiple traumatic events, often of an invasive, interpersonal nature, with a wide-ranging, long-term impact. This form of trauma typically involves a sense of threat to physical or emotional well-being. It can result from experiences of prolonged abuse, neglect, living in areas of war or crime, chronic domestic violence, and other forms of severe, repetitive stress. Unlike single-incident trauma, which is linked to a specific event, complex trauma usually occurs over a period of time, often begins in child-hood, and can occur throughout adulthood.

The effects of complex trauma are profound and can extend beyond the emotional and psychological realms to include physical, social, and existential impacts. Individuals who have experienced complex trauma may struggle with emotional regulation, have difficulties forming healthy relationships, and may exhibit symptoms of post-traumatic stress disorder (PTSD), anxiety, depression, and a variety of other mental health issues.

They might also experience difficulties with self-perception, such as feelings of shame or guilt. They can have an altered sense of the perpetrator, which may include a preoccupation with revenge or a paradoxical loyalty to the abuser. All of this was true for my mom.

And because it's still not an official diagnosis in The Diagnostic and Statistical Manual of Mental Disorders, therapists and physicians are left with challenging ways to circumvent the managed care system to provide proper and appropriate treatment.

Additionally, environmental stressors, specifically heavy metal toxicity, are known contributors to Alzheimer's. My mom was a cosmetologist, an industry known for its use of heavy metals such as aluminum, arsenic, cadmium, mercury, and nickel, just to name a few.

A 2022 study published in the International Journal of Environmental Research and Public Health found that compared to the general population, hairdressers have higher incidents of various diseases.

Another study published in 2022, this one by Frontiers in Pharmacology, found that metal accumulation can cause lifelong deterioration, including severe neurological problems. There is a strong association between accidental metal exposure and various neurodegenerative disorders, including

Alzheimer's disease (AD), the most common form of dementia that causes degeneration in the aged.

My brothers and I cared for Mom for twelve years until her death. The most maddening part of this was that she was still *there*, even though she eventually lost the ability to speak. My mom is one of the most significant *reasons* why I left the corporate world to become a therapist and why I'm writing this book.

Dementia and Alzheimer's are complicated diseases. I'm not trying to simplify my mom's case, but it's important to understand complex trauma and stress and how it affects brain function throughout our lives.

Other things that have been attributed to cognitive decline include inflammation, chronic stress, anxiety, depression, poor diet, lack of exercise, and more. I'm not an expert on cognitive disease, nor is this book about this topic. However, I am well-versed and positioned to talk about the giant elephant in the room that we are all ignoring: how chronic environmental, emotional, and mental stressors are killing us.

No one should be dying this way. The research is very clear on how stress, anxiety, depression, trauma, and burnout are affecting our physical and mental bodies. And it's clear what we need to do about it.

Enter the Hustle Culture

Let's begin with a question that seems almost sacrilegious in today's high-pursuit world: What if, in our incessant pursuit of success, we are racing in the wrong direction and constantly trying to solve the wrong problems? What if there is a way to achieve anything we want in life, to have, do, and be anything we can imagine – even beyond our wildest dreams – while creating a life that is harmonious, a little calmer, happier, and even more productive?

This book is not a denunciation of ambition or hard work; rather, it's an invitation to redefine what these concepts mean in a world that equates busyness with worthiness. It's a call to pause, reflect, and intentionally ask ourselves, "What are we doing!?"

Hustle culture has seduced us with its siren song of success, promising riches and recognition at the cost of our health, relationships, and peace of mind. But as we chase this ideal, we often find ourselves trapped in a cycle of perpetual busyness that leaves little room for the things that make life meaningful.

We delay fun and joy with touts of, "After I get through (this big project, the holidays, soccer season, this next goal), *then* let's meet for dinner and drinks!"

This book is a journey into the heart of the hustle culture—its origins, impact, and most importantly, how we can navigate its demands without losing ourselves. And if you've begun to lose yourself, how to find your way back. You'll read about real-life experiences of how stress, overwhelm, anxiety, depression, trauma, and burnout wreak havoc on our bodies, minds, and relationships.

We will explore the transformative power of radically caring for ourselves through a blend of stories, psychological insights, and practical tools. This isn't spa days and copious amounts of wine but a profound daily practice of caring for your mind, body, and soul.

I have used this process with my clients and myself to help disrupt the norm in a way that is revolutionary in its simplicity and energizing in its rebellion.

Welcome to your new life. Thank you for being here. Thank you for being curious and for investing in yourself. Thank you for demanding more for your life and for fighting against the grain of what you've been taught by your parents, your employer, your friends, and your doctor.

After nearly two decades of hustling in the corporate world, I changed course to become a mental health therapist specifically because I experienced firsthand the physical and mental health strain of constantly doing. And now, after many years of overcoming obstacles and setbacks, this book has finally come to life.

Let's find our way back to ourselves, one radical act of self-care at a time. It's an honor to guide you on this journey as you demand more for yourself and your life. Your new life starts here. Let's go.

Chapter 1
Radical Curiosity

> "Be less curious about people and more curious about ideas."
>
> — Marie Curie

In the stillness of the night, a sudden, stabbing pain in my back shattered the silence, pulling me from the depths of sleep into a harsh, unwelcome wakefulness. It was 2am. I jumped out of bed, convinced something had taken a bite of me. A spider? Oh, dear Lord, please don't be a spider in my bed! I jumped out of my Ikea bed intended for teenagers and frantically threw off the sheets as if I were digging someone out of quicksand. Where is that thing!?

A quick look at my right-side love handle revealed that my fears had come to life. A sequential line of red dots where the little bastard walked across me, taking little pieces as he went, like a soccer mom on the second day of the Whole 30 diet inhaling the last of the bits of salt and vinegar chips in the middle of the night.

The pain was unexpected and unyielding, a distress signaling something was wrong. As the fog of sleep cleared and I could collect my thoughts fully, I stood there and laughed. Hard. I figured I probably wouldn't die, so I took some Benadryl and went back to bed.

A few days went by, and the line of red dots wasn't getting any worse, but it wasn't getting any better, either. I took myself to the urgent care to get checked out "just in case." I walked in there with bold confidence, ready to tell the doctor my diagnosis, ask for a steroid shot, and I'd be on my way. I pulled up my shirt and tugged down my yoga pants just far enough to reveal the love handle. "Hey doc, I got bit by something, see?"

The doctor took one look and said, "that's shingles."

Um, what?! I see the shingles vaccine commercials for people 30 years older than me. I was 37 at the time. There's a mistake. This is a spider bite… or something. Nope, it was shingles. The doctor drew on me with a sharpie to mark the edges so we would know if it got worse.

He then made me wear a mask as I left the office and told me to go home to quarantine. This was years before COVID, so the thought of quarantine was so utterly foreign that my boss didn't believe me. Maybe he'll read this book and know that I, indeed had shingles.

I spent the first few days in disbelief—mad, even. I had no other symptoms—nothing, nada. Not a fever, not a headache, not an upset stomach—nothing. I felt… fine. My frustration slowly subsided, and eventually, as I regained rational thoughts, I began to get curious.

Everything I searched online pointed to "older adults who had chickenpox virus when they were young." Getting shingles in your 30s is so rare that I struggled to find statistics on it. What I did find pointed to one probable cause: stress. I took a hard look at my life. I didn't feel stressed. I felt "regular."

Shingles, as I would learn, was not just a rash or temporary discomfort. It was a tangible manifestation of stress, a physical representation of the relentless pressure and hustle that had become my norm. The virus lay dormant, a silent spectator to my daily internal battles, until the perfect storm of stress, anxiety, and overwhelm provided it the stage it needed to emerge in full force. This episode was more than a wake-up call; it was a confrontation with the unsustainable pace of my life. It forced me to confront myself – literally in the mirror.

As I navigated the painful weeks of recovery, I was compelled to reflect on the choices that led me here. But, like most of us, I am a slow learner, and the intrusive, ruminating thoughts that dominated my crushing anxiety were, at this time, stronger than my capacity to heal.

This is why my friend Erin texted me a few months later, *"Are you going to Valerie's Halloween party?"* I immediately went into off-the-rails internal dialogue of all the reasons why I didn't want to go. My mind was rushed with excuses and a battery of negative thoughts. The anxiety was louder than ever.

It was October 2014, a full two and a half years since I separated from my husband and a full one and a half years since our divorce was final. I had bought myself a cute little condo where I could lick my wounds and begin rebuilding my life. This is not a pretty tale that can be told in ninety minutes of a rom-com.

It wasn't pretty at all. It was messy. And hard. And embarrassing. And confusing. And complicated. Instead of a music montage of me getting a new hair style and upgrading my wardrobe, and getting my groove back, what actually happened on most days was far uglier and very, very real.

Usually, I closed the curtains, ate fast food for dinner, drank wine by myself, and watched Hallmark movies in the dark. That's not entirely true. Sometimes, I watch Dateline because we all know few things are more soothing than the sound of Keith Morrison's voice. I was convincing myself that my life would never look like the plot of *Summer at the Vineyard.*

I was not someone who quit her big corporate job to return home to run the family farm while reuniting with the love of her life. That was far too simplistic. Real life is way more complicated, dreadful, and difficult to manage, especially during very dark times. You know, like divorcing when you're in your 30s.

Even though Erin and I are the same age, I knew that the average age of people attending the party would be at least five years younger than us. The thought of going to the party being a 37-year-old divorcee made me feel like an old spinster. But which was worse? Going to this party as a pariah or the thought of spending one more second alone in that condo?

Spending another night with the curtains drawn while I drank in the dark alone was a far heavier and scarier burden to bear. So, after wrestling for more than 45 minutes with what should have been a very simple question, I finally responded to Erin with a simple "yes."

This decision would eventually change not only my life but the lives of several others. I opened the curtains, put myself in the shower, and prepared for the party. Since it was a Halloween party, I couldn't just wear jeans and a T-shirt. The thought crossed my mind: *What if no one dresses in costume and I show up like Elle Woods wearing a bunny outfit, while everyone else is dressed like a normal adult, and my ex-husband is there?* Do I even have anything that could be a costume?

Maybe I could find something like an old beach towel and fashion it into a cape! And then I could grab my eye mask from the drawer, cut eye holes in it, and strap it to my face. I could be a superhero called DIVORCE-O! whose superpowers include intrusive thoughts, trauma bonding, and crippling anxiety. That sounds like a fun costume.

Instead, I chose one that would make me feel slightly less terrible about myself, instead of emphasizing my weakest points. I looked in my closet and saw my red bandanna. I stuck that in my hair, put on a denim shirt and hot red lipstick, and viola! – Rosie the Riveter.

I had decided that I would have a good time that night, and there was no turning back. So DIVORCE-O on the inside and Rosie on the outside, I strutted into that party, poured myself a beer from the garage keg, and exhaled.

I knew just about everyone at this party, more or less, and I was having a great time guessing some costumes and complimenting others' creativity. It felt good to be out among people instead of sitting at home doom-scrolling social media in the dark. And I realized that most people at this party either didn't know I was divorced or they didn't care. The stress and overthinking were mostly inside my own head.

This was an indoor-outdoor party as the weather permitted, and I found myself standing in the driveway when I saw one of my co-workers who asked me if I was Amelia Earhart. Everyone standing around us had a great laugh at the American education system. I made a mental note to dress as Amelia for next Halloween.

Just then I saw a very tall, handsome, bald man staring at me, laughing. He said, "hi, Rosie!" as we cheered our red solo cups together. It was warm that year for October so he was dressed in a simple polo shirt and a pair of shorts. A sweater was tied around his shoulders and he held a tennis racket. He looked like a character from a 1980s romantic comedy. I laughed judgingly and said, "it looks like you spent about as much time on your costume as I spent on mine!"

We ended up chatting for the rest of the night, just the two of us standing in that same spot at the corner of the driveway. His name was Stefan and he had just returned to the United States after teaching English as a Second Language in Korea. I shared that I had spent some time studying abroad in undergraduate school. As I was saying this, I realized my study abroad was a full 11 years prior, and…here come the intrusive thoughts!

"My goodness, I was an undergrad 11 years ago!? God, I'm old. I am divorced. I am a loser." We continued chatting. He asked me who I knew at the party, why I was there, and who invited me by asking cutely, "how do you know these jokers?"

This was mostly a superficial conversation and we took small breaks to play a couple of rounds of beer pong in the garage. We didn't exchange information or anything, but we did agree to become friends on social media, as one does in 2014.

The last time I dated was in college in the late 90s/early 2000s, a time when people left each other voicemails on their home answering machines. The rules have changed now. Instead of asking for my phone number, some guy sent me a friend request on Facebook. Good Lord, how old am I?

As the night ended, I found Valerie, told her what a great time I had at the party, and thanked her for inviting me. By this time, it was after 1am and everyone was slurring words and hugging with a big, "I love you, man!" Accordingly, I told her I loved her and that some really handsome guy was flirting with me all night. She laughed as she couldn't think of any single people there (ouch).

Through a haze of keg-beer, I briefly thought I imagined the entire night. When I told her it was Stefan, she screeched the way sorority girls do when it's been five minutes since they've seen each other. Then she quickly said, "oh my goodness, you and Stefan are perfect for each other, but I never thought about connecting you because he lives out of town!"

Okay, okay, let's calm down. He doesn't live here. We're not exchanging numbers. It was simply a great night. I had a giant smile on both the outside and the inside for the first time in a long time, not that I'm suggesting anyone should rest their happiness or value as seen by a romantic interest.

However, it was the first time in almost 3 years that I felt hopeful. Not hopeful of 'landing a man' but hopeful that life is on the other side of a major transition such as divorce. I was far from some big epiphany. But I was slowly beginning to be ready to open the curtains and maybe stop eating fast food as often. And maybe only drinking socially. It was gradual, but it was a start. I've never been one to attach my success in life on attention from a man, but at this point, it felt really good to just simply let my hair down to enjoy the present moment without attaching any other meaning around it.

Stefan and I became friends on Facebook. He lived four hours away. I still wasn't interested in dating someone seriously, and he still wasn't asking me out, so I enjoyed getting to know this person as much as I could from afar. For the most part, I put him out of my mind. So, I told everyone goodnight, and I left the party alone.

As fall gave way to winter, I settled into a pattern of work and home. Work and home. Work and home. I was making healthier choices in terms of alcohol and food consumption. I completely stopped my social cigarette habit. I even returned to practicing yoga, something I loved but had gotten away from for a while. I decorated my tiny place for fall with a cornucopia and pillows that were burnt orange.

Of course, I was still watching the Hallmark Channel daily, so home décor inspiration was bountiful! Later, I even put up a Christmas tree and hung lights around the wrought iron railing on my teeny tiny balcony. I spent a lot of time on that balcony, even in winter. It overlooked a golf course, and the view was nice all year long.

There was a statue in front of the golf course. My balcony faced directly towards it, so directly that it appeared as if the statue was staring at me. The statue is of a woman from the pioneer days when Americans first settled in the West.

She is dressed in a bonnet, a long dress, and boots that look like the 18th-century version of Doc Martens. A toddler or small child clings tightly to her skirt. She carries a baby in one arm and a rifle in the other. I began to get curious about her. Who is she? Where is she going? Are those her children? Why does she need that weapon? Her face is determined, and her gaze is steady.

My curiosity led me to research her. Her name is *Madonna of the Trail* and she is one of twelve statues placed along the old national road from Cumberland, Maryland to Upland, California. They were commissioned by the National Society of Daughters of the American Revolution. Combined with the concrete foundation, she stands nearly 18 feet tall.

And get this: she is meant to represent a "symbol of the courage and faith of the women whose strength and love aided so greatly in conquering the wilderness and establishing permanent homes" (Wikipedia, 2023). So, while I'm sitting here in a sad condo, I am constantly reminded to have courage, strength, tenacity, and resilience. I began to wonder if the wilderness I needed to conquer was that of my own mind.

I found myself beginning to stare at her daily. I began talking to her. Was she trying to talk to me? What was she trying to communicate? Was she precisely the vision I needed to find the courage within myself to keep going? What else could I learn about myself from her?

Now, before you start thinking, "okay, she's lost it. She's talking to statues!" stay with me here for a moment. Remember, a few months earlier, I was so stressed that I gave myself shingles, and I was in a loop of eating terrible food, drinking alone, and scrolling social media in the dark while I felt sorry for myself. And now, because of this mysterious woman and her children, I began to get curious. At first, I was curious about her. Then, I was inspired by her. Then, I started to get curious about myself.

What was *I* capable of? The thought of her journey was simultaneously daunting and the most inspiring thing I had ever seen. Think about it. She quite literally blazed a trail where there was none. The rifle could double as a hatchet, clearing the way so those who came after her would have an easier path. I could not imagine a journey into unknown territory with two small children in tow. How did she care for these children? What resources did she have? She just found and created what she needed for herself along the way. What began as a mild curiosity about the history of the American pioneer woman turned into a small spark being lit inside of me.

I had no idea how this statue and I would eventually have so much in common.

What is Curiosity?

Before we discuss why curiosity is so important and how it can change our lives forever, we must first understand what curiosity is. A good place to begin learning about curiosity is by looking to children as they are the perfect specimens for studying curiosity and mindfulness.

Children are ever-present in all they do, solely focused on the task at hand. They are also endlessly interested in everything. They are the consummate question askers. What is this? What is that? How does this work? And, of course, every parent's favorite: Why?

Somewhere between childhood and adulthood, we begin to have life experiences that change us. The inevitable experiences we all have in life will eventually dampen things like creativity so that our primal brains can focus on survival. We enter survival mode, also known as flight-fight-freeze, and stay there—sometimes forever. Even worse, we begin to become conditioned to what psychologists call the external locus of control.

This is the idea that happiness comes from something outside of ourselves. We start to believe that certain foods or people or, shopping or, sex or experiences are what bring us joy. We say things like, "I'm eating this donut because I deserve it!" while simultaneously declaring this is the year we will finally lose the weight for good. You'll read more about this later, but for now, let's begin by understanding how asking the right questions at the right time can lead you to places you didn't even realize you wanted or needed to go.

Without discussing Dr. Judson Brewer, I can't possibly write a book about curiosity and pressing pause. Dr. Jud's ground-breaking work in the fields of anxiety and addiction has changed the way we think about our approach to healing. His TED Talk, *A Simple Way to Break a Bad Habit*, has been viewed nearly 19 million times. His New York Times Best-Selling book *Unwinding Anxiety: New Science Shows How to Break the Cycles of Worry and Fear to Heal Your Mind*, has an entire chapter dedicated to the science of curiosity.

In it, he describes the two sides of curiosity of Pleasant and Unpleasant as termed by psychologists Jordan Litman and Paul Silvia in 2006. The pleasurable side of curiosity is called *interest,* or I-curiosity while the unpleasant side is called *deprivation,* or D-curiosity. Deprivation curiosity happens when there is an almost primal need for information. In this state, the ancient part of our brain tries to fill in holes or gaps in knowledge.

Dr. Jud teaches us that this is why we search the internet for information about an actor while watching a movie. Our brains *must* know where we saw this actor before. He also explains why we *must* check our phones when a text comes in. The need to know the answer overrides our ability to remain in a state of uncertainty.

What I am most interested in is curiosity—the state we are in when we are in a desirable state for learning something. Dr Jud states, "It turns out curiosity builds on rewards-based learning. Rewards-based learning relies on positive and negative reinforcement. You want to do more things that feel good and less things that feel bad." More importantly, with interest and curiosity, the answers we seek are found within ourselves and, therefore, will never run out. With deprivation and curiosity, the answers we seek are external; therefore, no matter how much we seek things, we will never be satiated. This is the hallmark of both addiction and healing.

What does this mean for you? Most people walk around daily without being aware of themselves at any particular moment. Both types of curiosity can work together in harmony to help us begin to become aware of ourselves. By pressing pause on our day (more on this later in the book), we can slowly come to curiosity, which, as you'll learn, can lead to a greater sense of healing than anyone previously thought possible.

Deprivation curiosity happens when you feel a weird feeling in your stomach, and you simply must know what it is right now.

Hence, you turn to Google or frantically scroll social media searching for answers. Your need-to-know leads you down some wild paths, where after a while of playing manic detective, you're convinced you have exactly six minutes to live.

It's just then you remember hearing about your college roommate's cousin who had 'stomach pains' and they ended up needing emergency surgery, so that's it. This is most likely what's happening to you. The stimulus or activation point is the weird pain, the automatic behavior is doom scrolling and, finally, the result is anxiety.

Interest curiosity, on the other hand, is feeling some anxiety starting to creep in (or come on suddenly) and becoming curious without wanting to do anything about it. By simply taking a moment or two to press pause and tune into your body, your attention gets directed away from anxious feelings and into a deeper realm of tapping into the physical sensations of the body. This brings you out of your head and back into your body with a sense of grounding and safety.

Try this the next time anxiety rears its ugly head and tries to hijack your day. Becoming open to curiosity and allowing your mind to experiment with interest and wonder rather than a need for a solution creates a whole world of possibilities you didn't even realize were there. The stimulus is the same, aka stomach pain, but now the behavior has evolved from doom scrolling to curiosity, with the final result being a reduction in anxiety.

Practical Self-Care Tools, Resources, and Exercises

I invite you to get curious about how curiosity can help you in your life. The very first step in any behavior change, healing process, goal setting, or mindset shift begins with curiosity. Did my life magically change because I met a guy at a party? Nope. What happened instead was far more transformative.

I began to get curious. I used a combination of deprivation curiosity and interest curiosity to take a deeper dive into my health and my potential. Do I still get crippling anxiety? Yep. However, the art of curiosity provides us with the framework for questioning our own perceptions about the world within us so that we can change our relationship with our intrusive thoughts, anxiety, and stress.

Ways to get curious:

1. **Disrupt your intrusive thoughts with curiosity.** When you begin to notice yourself going off the rails with intrusive thoughts, anxiety, or stress – first stop and make the "hmmmm" sound. Then start asking questions: What is this really about? What is actually true here? What else is true about this situation? How much of this is simply being made up by my own mind?
2. **Stop the overwhelm.** Too much is too much, and it's important to remember that. When you start getting

curious, go slowly and know when to stop. If you get too caught up in the situation, your autonomic nervous system will shut down because it will be overloaded.

3. **Keep your mind and your options open.** When we're overwhelmed, it's common to be closed off to options. We get stuck in our story, and our primal brain wants to stay there because it feels protective and safe. However, true growth comes when we're able to intentionally choose higher-level thinking. Said more clearly, curiosity opens us up to the greatest gift of all—possibility.

Chapter 2
Creating Chaos
Unraveling the History of the Hustle Culture

"If you're always trying to be normal, you will never know how amazing you can be."

— Maya Angelou

Spring is my favorite time of year. The damp and dark of winter give way to warmth and sunlight. The days are longer. The earth and people seem to come alive after a season of wintering. Springtime is the season of renewal. It's the season of weddings, graduations, and picnics.

It beckons us to begin anew, to step into a season of rebirthing in which we come out of the shadows and awake into softness. It's also my literal birthday season.

By the spring of 2015, I began noticing significantly positive changes in myself. Although I still had bad days of overwhelming stress, crippling anxiety, and loads of self-doubt, generally I was more upbeat. Overall, I was more peaceful underneath. I began meditating for the first time. I had no idea what I was doing, so I used an app that featured Oprah and Deepak Chopra.

I had purchased the condo to start over after my divorce, and now, three years later, I have begun dreaming of what might be next. The condo association didn't allow pets, and I really wanted a dog and a yard. Curiosity led me to dream of what might be possible in different areas of my life, and I thought about what it would take to buy a house.

In addition to being naturally curious, I am a master at goal-setting and manifesting dreams. I am a person who will never be deterred and who always gets back up no matter how low or off-track I get. I am also the queen of creating my own chaos. The hard truth is that you create your own chaos, too. It's no wonder I was led into a career path of helping other people understand and manage their stress because I am the master of creating my own stress too. And we all do this to some degree. We continually create chaos in our lives. The challenge is that it's very difficult to admit this to ourselves.

We spend a lot of energy focusing on the external factors that might be at play and very little time getting real with ourselves about our role regarding the stress in our lives. I realize this might be very triggering for you, or you might be saying to yourself, *but what about this big terrible thing that happened to me!?*

If you're having those thoughts as you're reading this, that is simply resistance rearing its ugly head. Getting curious about and becoming aware of our resistance when triggered is the first step to healing. When you hear things like, "hey, you might be the creator of the chaos in your life," it's completely normal for the next thought to be, "you don't know my life, lady! Why are you trying to tell me everything is my fault!"

This is not about placing blame or telling you that the bad things in your life are your fault. However, we do create stress and chaos in our own lives when we take on more than is necessary. We take on extra projects, especially regarding work, because we want to show up as a good employee.

We want to show up as the good sibling, the good partner, the good daughter, son, and a good friend so we continually take on things that are way beyond our capacity to handle at any given moment.

I was determined to climb out from the seemingly bottomless hole of chaos I had dug myself over the previous three years. To do this, I had to get brutally honest with myself. Not only did I dig my own hole, but I went down to the hardware store myself to buy the shovel. Now it was time to build a ladder to climb out of the mess I had made.

I am the reason I am divorced. I am the reason I am lonely. I am the reason I'm stuck. I'm the reason I'm broke. I'm the reason I've gained weight. This is a harsh reality.

Sometimes we must look in the mirror and face the fact that we are the cause of the internal chaos. It's so easy to blame outside factors, i.e., other people. During this time of my life, I was unable to see myself in these terms, so of course, I kept blaming all the other things. And even though some things were slowly improving, there was still much emotional work to complete.

Doing things is my way through to the other side of whatever I am faced with. This is true for so many of us. Our primal brain, driven to protect and keep us safe, defaults to the lowest setting and keeps us stuck. Stuck in our ways, stuck in our patterns, and stuck in our minds. So, we keep busy to prevent our higher-thinking selves from having to deal with the storm surrounding us. And so was the case here.

I was working my full-time job, which I really enjoyed. The people with whom I worked were fantastic, the salary was one with which I could live. It wasn't going to make me a millionaire, but it was a doable, livable salary, especially for the place in the country where I was based. I had health insurance and a small retirement account.

There were two things I couldn't shake: the gut feeling that there *had* to be a way for me to afford to buy a house and this nagging feeling inside that there was more to life than...*this*. Things were good, I suppose, but something was missing.

So, in addition to the full-time job, I decided to get a real estate license. My brother is a realtor. He's very successful, and his business is growing, so he was sort of nudging me towards it. In addition, he could have used the extra help. The idea was that I could sort of just do it on the weekends by helping him with open houses and things like that.

I thought, "okay, maybe I can make a few extra bucks and, at best, I really only have to work a couple of hours on a Sunday. Let's do it!" Much to my surprise, I really enjoyed selling real estate. Several people in my family are involved in real estate —both residential and commercial—including both of my brothers and one of my uncles. If we had a family business, it would be buying, selling, and developing real estate.

I ended up selling over $1 million worth of real estate in one year, working less than part-time in a very small market. At the year's end, the realtors board has an awards dinner. And much to the shock of everyone – mostly myself – I received an award for Rookie of the Year. I'm not saying I didn't work hard, but it seems preposterous that someone working less than part-time would be able to produce that much in year one.

I was also teaching college classes part-time as an adjunct instructor at my alma mater and of course I couldn't just teach one class. I was teaching two classes, both of which were in-person in the evenings. During the day I was working my full-time career, the evenings were spent teaching college classes, and on the weekends I was selling houses.

While this had a positive impact on my bank account and kept my mind off the real work (my mental health), it created an enormous amount of stress. At this time in my life, I had unhealed trauma and didn't have the first clue about stress or anxiety or how any of this worked or affected me. I just kept going and going and going to the point of completely breaking down. And that's precisely what happened.

Some of it was enjoyable, however I certainly wasn't ever planning anything fun for myself. I wasn't planning vacations or spending any quality time with friends. On the outside it appeared as if I was killing it by the American standard for defining success. I was doing so good *financially* rebuilding my life that I ignored everything else.

My alarm would go off thirty minutes before I had to be at work. It took everything I had to get out of bed, brush my teeth, and put on a clean dress. Every day my life was like that Bangles song from the 1980s called *Manic Monday*; "*...if I had an aeroplane, I still wouldn't make it on time.*" I. Was. Exhausted. Mentally. Emotionally. Physically.

I still had not fully dealt with the repercussions from the divorce. I hadn't fully dealt with the issues that led to the divorce in the first place. I was just go-go-go and was oscillating between overachieving and isolation. Producing and shutting down. Being "on" out in the world, and being totally "out" when I was home. I was not only doing what researchers call pendulating between fight and freeze, but I was being praised for it.

I was winning all these awards: Rookie of the Year (board of Realtors®) 40 under 40, Outstanding Young West Virginian. I even won an award called Wonder Woman. A lot of people were celebrating me for my professional success while in reality I was a total fucking disaster and, frankly, felt like a fraud.

I've always loved live music. I even played in a rock band for a while in my 20s. One night I went to my favorite place to see one of my favorite bands with some of my favorite people. I loved everything about this scene. It's one I've experienced thousands of times.

The crowd is wound up and ready for a great time. The drinks are flowing. I can taste the Corona Light now. I'm wearing something that makes me feel fierce and free. It's too loud to talk – perfect for hiding out in public. We were on the dance floor in full tilt.

Everyone is a little drunk and a little sweaty as we jump together in synchronicity, screaming the lyrics and pointing to each other as if to say, "THIS LYRIC GETS US! MUSIC IS LIFE!"

It was just then that something began to happen to me. I got tunnel vision as if I was having an out-of-body experience. Everything sort of went quiet. I couldn't breathe. I felt like I was choking. I felt my chest compressing. My hands were sweating. And I had an overwhelming feeling that I HAD TO GET OUT OF THERE IMMEDIATELY.

My friend walked out to the parking lot with me. I said, "something is very wrong. I need to go to the ER." She remained calm and drove me there. All I could think about was that my mom nearly died from pulmonary embolisms around the same age that I was at this moment and her symptoms were eerily similar. I just kept thinking over and over, "this is it. I don't think I'm going to make it."

The ER doctor came in to assess me. The doc was someone I went to high school with and I thought, "she's a doctor and my life is a disaster – great." She asked, "have you been under any stress lately?" To which I vehemently declared, "no. It's blood clots in my lungs. Is it blood clots in my lungs!?"

The person who accompanied me to the ER broke into the conversation and was nearly laughing. "Um....she's recently completed a leadership program, switched jobs, finished a master's degree, and got a divorce." The doc, without judgment, sat down next to me, took my hand, and said, "honey, you've had a panic attack."

The History of the Hustle

Welcome to the hustle culture! In today's fast-paced society, we are bombarded with messages that glorify busyness and productivity. It seems like everyone is always on the go, striving to do more and achieve more. But in the midst of this hustle and bustle, we often overlook the importance of slowing down and taking care of ourselves.

It's easy to get caught up in the never-ending cycle of work, deadlines, and obligations. We feel pressure to constantly move forward and to be doing something productive. Moreover, we thrive in the hustle. We actually enjoy this pace. But it's crucial to remember that our well-being is just as vital as our achievements.

The roots of the hustle culture run deep, stemming from societal norms that value productivity above all else. We're conditioned to equate busyness with success and to believe that we must always be hustling to get ahead. This mentality can take a toll on our mental health as we push ourselves to the brink in pursuit of external validation. But the high cost of constant busyness is undeniable.

Burnout, anxiety, and exhaustion are common byproducts of the hustle culture. We sacrifice our well-being at the altar of productivity, neglecting our physical and emotional needs in the process.

Have you ever stopped to get curious about how this all started and where it comes from? We might guess from the previous generation who taught us the value of a hard day’s work. Well, who taught them this value? It must the generation before them. In fact, it actually goes all the way back to the late nineteenth and early twentieth centuries.

Famed psychiatrist William S. Sadler wrote about a little-understood medical issue that seemed to affect physical health and the nervous system. Seeing a rise in cardiovascular disease, high blood pressure, and stroke, Sadler grouped these conditions together and called it Americanitis.

He wrote that this is due to "the hurry, bustle, and incessant drive of the American temperament." A *Time* magazine article from 1925 wrote about a talk Sadler gave in which it was noted that the number of U. S. citizens annually hurrying, bustling, and driving themselves to death was set at 240,000. This was in 1925 – 99 years prior to the time I am writing this book. Americanitis has also been defined as "excessive nervous tension."

It also has origins to the medical term *Neurasthenia,* which became a diagnosis in the late nineteenth and early twentieth centuries, believed to affect the upper class and professionals working in sedentary environments. This is from too much stress, not enough sleep, not eating properly, not getting enough exercise, etc. The cure back then? Rest. Hmmmm….

Benefits of Ambition and Drive

One important thing to note here is that I am not suggesting the hustle is a bad thing. We're not trying to assign names like 'good' or 'bad' to any of this – we're simply naming it for what it is – there *is* indeed a hustle culture. That said, there are myriad benefits of ambition and drive.

One of the most obvious benefits of the hustle is financial gain, security, and freedom. Isn't the American dream to buy a house and 'have it all'? Well, the hustle is the main way we achieve that. Working hard means we can adequately provide for our family.

There is a primal need for survival; once that is satisfied, then we move into the desires of consumerism, philanthropy, and wealth-building. These are noble and exciting aspirations. Want a beach house? Work hard and you'll get it! Ah... America.

Another substantial benefit of the hustle is a sense of self-achievement. Accomplishing goals for ourselves and/or for the companies who employ us gives a dopamine rush and a sense of pride. We might even be recognized with an award at the annual dinner or maybe even a promotion. Huzzah! I have personally been honored with several awards throughout my career and guess what – it feels fantastic!

Other benefits include things like leadership development – want to be in the C-Suite one day? Hustling could get you there. From the time we are young children we are inundated with messages – both direct and subtle – that we can be anything if we work hard enough. And let's not forget about resiliency and grit. Learning to become resilient is not just an effective coping mechanism, it is an important part of our character.

Resiliency gives us confidence in ourselves. It gives us coping skills so that when the next thing happens, we bounce back a little faster. It gives us a pathway to help us lean into our core values. It's been said that our character isn't built during tough times but rather, it's revealed through how we respond to challenges. This is one of the most important benefits of the hustle.

Societal Impacts of Glorifying Busyness

What do you say when someone asks how you are? Do ever answer with, "good. Busy. Good." In a 2023 Harvard Business Review article, Adam Waytz discusses an experiment that was conducted to find out how people answer this question. The study, conducted by performance coaching firm Hintsa, found that nearly eight out of ten people answered this question with "busy." Oof. We have some work to do, folks.

In some countries, like France and Italy, leisure time is considered a status symbol. Long lunches, intentional time with friends, being outdoors, and taking naps are all deemed to be admirable. In the U.S., conversely, someone with a jam-packed schedule is seen as a model employee and marking that you 'must be important' and that you're out-performing others with your 'I don't need that much sleep' mentality.

The social psychology term *effort justification* is the idea that we value an outcome more the harder we've worked for it. The paradigm here is that we also have something known as cognitive dissonance. Cognitive dissonance is the theory that we change our attitudes about something to reduce how uncomfortable it truly is.

Let's unpack all this for just a second. Let's say you are experiencing a very tough time at work. You're putting in long hours working in a demanding job. The pressure is mounting. You start to feel a little resentment, irritation or even anger towards your boss, the company leadership, or co-workers. You swear that as soon as you 'get through' this project or busy season you're going to start looking for a new position. Then, the project ends, or the busy season starts to balance out and you're rewarded with a huge financial bonus or trip to a luxury resort. Your friend checks in to see how you're doing.

And your tone has changed. You might say something like, "oh, I'm good. Better now that the busy season is winding down. I won a trip this quarter!" And when your friend reminds you that you were manically updating your resume only last week, you remark, "it's all good. This place isn't actually that bad. I'm going to stick it out. I think I'll get promoted soon." This is cognitive dissonance tied to effort justification.

Values

Why do we do this and what can we do to reverse this cycle for ourselves? We can begin to move in a different direction by using curiosity to understand our values. Values work is one of my favorite things to explore with therapy clients and corporate wellness clients alike.

Many people don't take the time to truly define and understand their values; but when you do, magic can happen. One of the approaches I use in therapy is ACT: Acceptance and Commitment Therapy. Values work is fundamental to ACT skills. In this context, Values help us get curious about ourselves.

We ask ourselves questions such as: What really matters to you on a deep level? What do you want to do with your one short and precious life? What sort of person do you want to be? What characteristics or qualities do you want to embody?

Practical Tools and Exercises for Nurturing Ambition and Inspired Action

There's nothing like some easy breezy existentialism to start your day! Values work doesn't have to be that heavy, so let's make this easy. The first step is defining values. I'll give you an outline of how that works in a bit. The second step is understanding why each value is important to you.

When you're clear on your why, things like motivation, consistency, decision making, and boundaries become considerably easier. That is because we're not "motivated" by emotions (i.e., I'm too tired to go to the gym) but rather we are driven by what matters most to us (i.e., I get up early and workout because I value my health). The latter makes the former nonexistent.

How do we go about defining values? Here is a simple values exercise to get you started.

Step 1: Take out a piece of paper and a pen. Yes, actual paper and pen. Nothing electronic.

Step 2: Draw a vertical line down the center of the paper. On the left side of the vertical line, draw three horizontal lines. Repeat this on the right side.

Step 3: On the left side, write the name of someone you admire (one on each line) for a total of three names. This can be someone you know, someone you don't know, a historical figure (like Alexander Hamilton), a fictional character (like Wonder Woman), or an idea of a person (like author, female entrepreneurs, athlete, musician, artist, etc.).

Step 4: On the right side, write three things you admire about each person. You should have a total of nine characteristics (3 for each of the 3 people). An example would be: Oprah: kind, generous, trailblazer.

Step 5: Once you've completed this, cover up the names on the left side so that all you can see are the characteristics. This is a list of Values that you either **desire** to embody…or you **already do but aren't living in alignment** with your values.

The final step is to spend time contemplating **why** each value is important to you. The key here is that the why must resonate deeply with you. The kind of feeling that you feel in your bones. No matter what life throws at you, you'll be able to bounce back (hello resilience!) with ease because of your values.

And when you start to get caught up in the chaos, get curious and check in with your values. Doing this will pull you out of stress and anxiety because it stands as your guidepost for what to do next, allowing you to create enough capacity to process and release your overwhelm, and to remember why you're doing what you're doing. This is how you come out of chaos and thrive in the hustle.

Chapter 3
Press Pause

"Don't spend time beating on a wall, hoping to transform it into a door."

— Coco Chanel

I used to work for a large electric utility company. We would often have planned power outages for equipment repair. We would contact customers via an automated phone system, notifying them that their power would be out on a specific day and time, such as Tuesday from 9am until 2pm. This is mildly inconvenient and a little irritating, but was necessary to fix old, outdated, or rundown equipment.

Here's the thing – the equipment was old and needed to be repaired or replaced. The company *could* say, "yeah, we should probably look at that but we don't have time right now – we'll deal with it later." The latter usually results in an unplanned or unexpected power outage that lasts significantly longer, is more expensive to fix, puts line workers in danger, and pisses off the whole neighborhood.

The human body works in the same way. It is a magnificent machine, exquisitely designed with an internal communication system that outperforms the most sophisticated super computers in the world. Internal systems are constantly talking to each other, scanning for viruses, making auto-corrections when it spies a problem brewing, and sending reports back to the home office (you) notifying you that something needs your attention.

The problem is, we ignore and dismiss these messages, telling ourselves that we'll deal with them later because we "don't have time right now." Our body is continually trying to talk to us, to get our attention that the battery is low, that the filters need changing, and that if we don't take the time to stop and fix things, it will shut down completely. Much like the electric utility company, the latter results in unexpected and significantly longer down time, it costs us more, it's more severe, and it pisses us off.

This is precisely what happened when I had the panic attack. It was a very loud, very dramatic wake-up call. I was way out of balance. I spent most of Spring and Summer 2015 learning my own mind and listening to my body. I was still working towards goals such as buying a house, but I was doing it in a softer, less aggressive way. Well, what the hell does that mean?

I still needed the extra income to help with the goal of buying a house, but I realized that I was far more in control of my schedule than I previously thought. Up until the panic attack, I thought that if a potential buyer wanted to see a house then I had to say yes only to their availability. I thought I could only do open houses when I was asked to.

I thought if I said 'no' to teaching another college course or dropping down to only teaching one class that I would be blacklisted from the adjunct instructor roster. Turns out, none of those things were true at all.

Instead of responding IMMEDIATELY to a text or phone call in the real estate world, I would hit the pause button and allow myself some time to think it through. A buyer with whom I was working would send me a text with something to the effect of: "I saw that 717 Hamilton Avenue is on the market. I've always loved that street. Can we see it today at 4pm?"

The pre-panic attack me would've replied instantly with, "Yes! Let me contact the seller's agent to arrange it! I'll get back to you asap to confirm!" However, when I learned to press pause, my response would not have been immediate. I would first look at my schedule (within a reasonable timeframe) to see what would make me feel not-so-rushed.

Then, I would contact the seller's agent to carry out some recon to see how much interest the home is getting (sometimes in real estate you have to make quick moves and other times you can take your time). Then, I would ask to arrange to show the home to my client.

Lastly, I would reply to my client with, "That is such a beautiful neighborhood. I can see why you love it! I got some more information about this home. Today at 4pm doesn't work, but 6pm today is perfect. Does that work for you?"

There is an art to real estate when it comes to timing and setting boundaries (more on boundaries later); however, when the timing is right and when delivered in the right way, pressing pause and allowing space to think things through brings a sense of calm and far less pressure to the situation.

The outcome is the same whether I showed this particular house on this particular day at 4pm or 6pm, however showing it at 6pm made my day substantially less stressed and rushed. Are there times in the real estate world when time is of the essence? Absolutely. And there are also many times when it's not.

The same is true in any industry. There are times when you must respond immediately to what is happening around you or to what is being asked of you; and there are also times when you can effectively slow your day down a little bit. Learning this skill and leaning into the art of it is how I was able to continue the extra income streams with softened edges.

It was around this time I also deepened my meditation practice and began setting my alarm earlier so that I could have time to meditate first thing in the morning. This small, intentional change slowly started to have big impacts on my life. I noticed that I wasn't as rushed in the morning. I wasn't as tired. I wasn't as overwhelmed by the day ahead.

During this time, I also returned to practicing yoga; something I've done for many years but had neglected recently. Is that it? Is it as simple as just engaging in guided meditation to Oprah's voice in the morning before performing a couple of downward dogs in the afternoon and viola – I'm cured? This sure would be a short book if so!

Finding Peace in the Hustle-Dominated Culture

Have you ever stopped to think about why we are constantly drawn to the concept of hustle in today's fast-paced world? It seems like everywhere we turn, there's this unspoken pressure to always be busy, to always be striving for more. But why is that?

One major factor is the culture in which we live - the hustle culture is deeply ingrained in our society. From a young age, we are taught that success requires hard work and relentless effort. This belief is reinforced by media portrayals of successful individuals who have hustled their way to the top. We idolize those who work tirelessly, often overlooking the toll it takes on their well-being.

Think about it - social media bombards us with images of people hustling and grinding while always being on the move. We see influencers painting a glorified picture of perpetual busyness. The pressure to keep up can be overwhelming, leading us to believe that if we're not constantly hustling, we're falling behind.

But have you ever stopped to question the true cost of this relentless pursuit of success? Burnout, anxiety, and a sense of emptiness can all be byproducts of this hustle mentality. We sacrifice our mental and physical health in the name of success, often losing sight of what truly matters in the process.

Beyond external pressures, our own inner drive can also fuel our obsession with hustle. The desire for validation, recognition, and a sense of accomplishment can push us to keep pushing ourselves harder and harder. We chase after external markers of success, hoping that each achievement will bring us closer to fulfillment.

It's crucial to recognize that success is not a one-size-fits-all concept. It's about finding a harmony that works for you, that honors your well-being and personal values. True success is not just about what you achieve externally, but also about how you feel internally. It's about finding joy, fulfillment, and a sense of purpose in what you do, without sacrificing your health and happiness along the way.

This is another great place to use curiosity. Are you hustling because it brings you joy and aligns with your values, or are you doing it out of fear and external pressures? Not only is pausing okay, but it is also necessary to reassess your priorities and increase productivity, as well as your mental, emotional, and physical capacity for more.

A 2021 study published in the Kansas Journal of Medicine found that psychological well-being is the biggest predictor of employee engagement, happiness, and productivity. Let me say this is another way. Psychological well-being wasn't 'one of' the factors attributed to how well employees 'performed' but rather it was the number one predictor of productivity. This means that when you're stressed and overwhelmed and 'pushing through', you're actually performing worse than if you were taking care of yourself.

While it may seem counterintuitive, pausing or taking a break with the sole purpose of intentionally re-setting our autonomic nervous system actually increases our productivity and capacity for creativity, happiness, and deep meaningful connections with others.

The Difference Between Sleep and Rest

Raise your hand if you are tired no matter how much sleep you get. If you're like millions of Americans, you probably raised your hand. According to a study by the Institute of Medicine (US) Committee on Sleep Medicine and Research, an estimated 50 to 70 million Americans chronically suffer from a disorder of sleep and wakefulness, hindering daily functioning and adversely affecting health and longevity.

The cumulative long-term effects of sleep deprivation and sleep disorders have been associated with a wide range of deleterious health consequences including an increased risk of hypertension, diabetes, obesity, depression, heart attack, and stroke.

It stands to reason, then, that if you are tired no matter how much sleep you get, then more sleep is likely not the answer to your fatigue problem. What you probably need instead is rest. So, what's the difference between sleep and rest?

Sleep and rest are two fundamental components of a healthy lifestyle, often used interchangeably in everyday language. However, they represent distinct physiological and psychological states with unique benefits and purposes. Understanding the differences between sleep and rest can empower you to better manage your energy, improve focus, concentration, reactivity to stress, lower anxiety, improve depression, and pull you out from the functional freeze state (more on functional freeze in Chapter 4).

Sleep is a vital, complex biological process that occurs in cycles, involving various stages including REM (Rapid Eye Movement) and non-REM sleep. It is characterized by a reduced state of consciousness, diminished sensory activity, and inactivity of nearly all voluntary muscles. Sleep is essential for the body's repair, growth, and detoxification processes.

During sleep, the brain consolidates memories, processes information, and restores cognitive functions, making it crucial for learning, problem-solving, and emotional regulation.

Rest, on the other hand, is a broader concept that encompasses any activity that helps to relax the body and mind, reducing stress and fatigue without necessarily falling asleep. Rest can be active or passive. Active rest includes activities that are mentally or physically refreshing but require some degree of engagement, such as walking, reading, or practicing yoga.

Passive rest involves doing very little, such as sitting quietly and breathing deeply or meditating. Rest is about giving the body and mind a break from the stresses of daily life and can occur while awake. It's about rejuvenation and is not exclusively tied to the physical recovery processes that dominate sleep.

The most striking difference lies in the physiological processes that occur during sleep, which are not replicated at rest. Sleep involves specific brain wave patterns, hormone regulation, and biological processes essential for health and survival.

Rest, while beneficial for alleviating fatigue and stress, does not substitute the complex functions of sleep, such as memory consolidation and muscle repair.

Another significant difference is the level of consciousness and engagement. Sleep requires disengagement from the environment, leading to unconsciousness. Rest, however, can involve a range of consciousness levels, from full awareness during certain activities to a more relaxed, but still awake, state.

Both sleep and rest serve to rejuvenate the body and mind, but they do so in different ways. Sleep addresses the physical and neurological needs essential for survival and long-term health. Rest, while it can contribute to physical recovery, primarily provides mental and emotional rejuvenation.

It allows individuals to momentarily step away from the demands of life, reducing stress and enhancing well-being. While sleep and rest are intertwined in the broader context of relaxation and rejuvenation, they are distinct states with different physiological processes, levels of consciousness, and specific benefits.

Sleep is a non-negotiable biological necessity that supports physical health, brain function, and emotional well-being. Rest, in its various forms, offers a flexible means of reducing fatigue and stress, complementing sleep but not replacing its critical role in health. Understanding and prioritizing both sleep and rest in one's lifestyle is key to achieving optimal well-being.

Specific Tools for Better Sleep

What if your sleep is disrupted and you wake up throughout the night still feeling tired no matter how much sleep you get? Improving your nighttime routine can significantly enhance the quality of your sleep, making you feel more rested and rejuvenated each day. Here are some common causes of sleep disruptions, followed by ideas to establish a better nighttime routine.

Common Causes of Sleep Disruptions

1. **Stress and Anxiety:** Worries about work, school, health, or family can keep your mind active at night, making it difficult to sleep.
2. **Irregular Sleep Schedule:** Shift work, jet lag, or a fluctuating sleep schedule can disrupt your body's internal clock and affect your sleep quality.
3. **Poor Sleep Environment:** A room that's too hot, too cold, too noisy, or too bright can interfere with sleep. An uncomfortable mattress or pillows can also contribute to sleep disturbances.
4. **Technology Use:** The use of electronic devices before bed can disrupt your natural sleep cycle due to the blue light they emit.
5. **Consumption of Stimulants and Alcohol:** Caffeine and nicotine can prevent you from falling asleep or

disrupt sleep later in the night. Alcohol might make you feel sleepy at first but can lead to disturbed sleep later.

6. **Medical Conditions:** Conditions such as sleep apnea, restless legs syndrome, chronic pain, or acid reflux can disrupt sleep. Mental health disorders like depression and anxiety can also contribute to sleep problems. By addressing these potential disruptors and implementing a solid nighttime routine, you can significantly improve your sleep quality. Remember, small changes can have a big impact on how well you sleep and, consequently, your overall health and well-being.

Easy Steps for a Better Nighttime Routine

1. **Establish a Consistent Sleep Schedule:** Try going to bed and waking up at the same time every day, even on weekends. This helps regulate your body's internal clock and improves sleep quality.
2. **Create a Relaxing Bedtime Ritual:** Engage in calming activities before bed, such as reading, taking a warm bath, or practicing relaxation exercises. This signals to your body that it's time to wind down.
3. **Limit Exposure to Blue Light:** The blue light emitted by phones, tablets, and computers can

interfere with your ability to fall asleep. Try to avoid screens at least an hour before bedtime.

4. **Be Mindful of Your Diet:** Avoid large meals, caffeine, and alcohol close to bedtime. These can disrupt sleep or prevent you from falling asleep easily.
5. **Create a Comfortable Sleep Environment:** Ensure your bedroom is conducive to sleep—cool, quiet, and dark. If necessary, consider using earplugs, white noise machines, or blackout curtains.
6. **Exercise Regularly:** Regular physical activity can help you fall asleep faster and enjoy deeper sleep. However, avoid vigorous exercise close to bedtime as it might keep you awake.
7. **Manage Worries:** Try to resolve your worries or concerns before bedtime. Writing down what's on your mind can be a good way to transfer your thoughts and clear your mind.

A note of caution about sleep: If you are having trouble sleeping and it's affecting your daily functioning and health, please contact a healthcare provider and/or mental health therapist for specific help.

Specific Tools for Rest – The Press Pause Method

Press Pause is a method I've developed to help myself manage anxiety and also get deep, meaningful rest. I've used it myself for years and began using it with clients a couple of years ago.

This method is practical in its simplicity and can be undertaken from anywhere and at any time. It is an adaptation of the psychological interventions of progressive muscle relaxation (PMR) and body scan meditation. These tools are evidence-based and clinically informed. Before we learn Press Pause, I'd like to take a deeper dive into these concepts.

Progressive Muscle Relaxation (PMR) is a relaxation technique that involves the sequential tensing and then relaxing of different muscle groups in the body. This method is designed to help reduce physical tension and mental stress, often leading to improved sleep quality and overall relaxation.

Developed by American physician Edmund Jacobson in the early 20th century, PMR is based on the premise that mental calmness is a natural result of physical relaxation.

The Benefits and Uses of PMR

1. **Stress and Anxiety Reduction:** By reducing physical tension, PMR can also lower stress and anxiety levels, promoting a sense of calmness.

2. **Improved Sleep:** The relaxation induced by PMR can make it easier to fall asleep and improve its quality, making it a beneficial practice before bedtime.
3. **Pain Management:** PMR can help alleviate discomfort from chronic pain conditions by relaxing muscle tension.
4. **Enhanced Well-being:** Regular practice of PMR can lead to an overall sense of well-being and improved mental health. Progressive Muscle Relaxation is a simple yet effective technique that can be incorporated into your daily routine to promote relaxation, reduce stress, and improve sleep. By practicing regularly, you can harness the benefits of this powerful relaxation tool to enhance your physical and mental health.

Body scan meditation is a form of mindfulness meditation that involves paying attention to parts of the body and bodily sensations in a gradual sequence from feet to head. This practice is often used to reduce stress, improve well-being, and decrease tension in the body.

It encourages practitioners to scan their body in a methodical way, noting any sensations, tensions, or discomforts without trying to change them. The goal is to simply observe and become more aware of the body's experiences without judgment.

Jon Kabat-Zinn is a significant figure in popularizing mindfulness meditation in the Western world. He is the founder of the Mindfulness-Based Stress Reduction (MBSR) program at the University of Massachusetts Medical School. The program, which Kabat-Zinn developed in the late 1970s, integrates mindfulness meditation and yoga practices to help people manage stress, anxiety, pain, and illness.

Body scan meditation is a key component of MBSR and reflects Kabat-Zinn's approach to mindfulness. His work has been instrumental in bringing mindfulness into the mainstream of medicine and society, showing that mindfulness practices can have profound effects on mental and physical health. Kabat-Zinn's teachings emphasize being present in the moment and becoming aware of one's body and mind in a non-judgmental way, which are central principles in body scan meditation.

Jon Kabat-Zinn has authored several influential books on mindfulness, including *Wherever You Go, There You Are* and *Full Catastrophe Living*, which explore mindfulness concepts and practices in depth. Through his writings and the MBSR program, Kabat-Zinn has made mindfulness and practices like body scan meditation accessible to a broad audience, contributing significantly to their popularity and acceptance in wellness and medical communities.

Press Pause

1. **Start by Finding a Comfortable Position:** You can lie on your back on a comfortable surface or sit in a comfortable chair. If lying down, let your legs extend out, slightly apart, with your arms resting by your sides, palms facing up. If sitting, keep your back straight and your feet flat on the floor. The key element here is to make yourself as comfortable as you can. There is no "right way" to do this – only to do what feels good for you.
2. **Close Your Eyes or Soften Your Gaze Downward:** This can help reduce distractions and make it easier to focus on bodily sensations. You can use an eye pillow, towel, t-shirt, bandanna, or anything else to cover your eyes.
3. **Breathe Deeply and Relax:** Place one hand on the heart and one hand on the belly. Take a long, slow, deep breath in through your belly, your nose, and windpipe. It's helpful to make a quiet sound while doing this, like an ocean or how you might imagine Darth Vader's breathing.
4. **Focus on Your Body:** Begin at your feet and slowly move your attention through different parts of your body. Notice sensations like warmth, coolness, tension, pain, or relaxation without trying to change them.

5. **Move Up Through Your Body:** Gradually move your focus from one part of the body to the next—up through the legs, torso, arms, and head. Pay attention to each area for a few moments before moving on.
6. **Observe Without Judgment:** If you notice discomfort, tension, or other sensations, simply observe them without judgment. The goal is not to change the sensations but to become aware of them and to observe them.
7. **Use Your Breath:** You can imagine breathing into and out of various parts of your body, which can help deepen your sense of relaxation and awareness.
8. **Conclude Your Practice:** After you've scanned your entire body, take a few deep breaths, move your awareness to your hearing as you slowly bring in some external sounds. When you're ready, slowly open your eyes. Take a moment to notice your overall state and how your body feels.

Press Pause is an effective and efficient method of engaging the vagus nerve in the parasympathetic nervous system (more on this in Chapter 5). This is meant to be done slowly, building your practice overtime. Begin by setting a timer for 90-120 seconds. Then slowly work your way up to five and then ten minutes. Research suggests that thirty to forty-five minutes of this practice is as relaxing to the physical body as 2-3 hours of

REM sleep. When done regularly and on purpose Press Pause can meaningfully change your life.

It can be done in between meetings or during transitional times of day such as upon waking, before walking to the office, after leaving the office, after driving, after an argument or uncomfortable conversation, before returning home or before rejoining the family after work, after the kids go to bed, or as part of your nighttime routine as you prepare for bed.

You can do this in your car, your office, in line at the grocery store, your living room, or even a public restroom stall! There are throngs of people all over the place sitting in their cars doing this while their kids are at soccer practice. If you see someone sitting in their car with their hand on their heart and eyes closed, don't worry – they've probably just read this book and are practicing Press Pause!

You've been waiting for this! For someone to give you permission to take a break from work to spend intentional, meaningful time with your family. Someone to give you permission to stop taking your laptop with you to the beach and to stop "checking in" with work when you are off, out of the office, or on vacation. Someone to give you permission to take a break from the kids to have lunch with your friends. Someone to give you permission to take a break from your friends when you need some time for yourself. Well, this is it.

This is your permission to step away, to check in with yourself, to intentionally calm your overworked nervous system, and to press pause.

Chapter 4
Your Hustling Brain
Psychological Costs of the Hustle

"When I hear somebody sigh, 'Life is hard,' I am always tempted to ask, 'Compared to what?'"

— Sydney Harris

By the fall of 2015, my anxiety was under control, the panic had disappeared, and my life seemed to be finding a nice groove that felt far less rushed and was loaded with relaxation and time with friends. Before the divorce, I was very involved in my community but had taken a step back in order to heal. Now I was ready to come out of hiatus and rejoin those things I enjoyed.

I was attending a charity fundraiser and truly having a great time when out of the blue I received a text message from my friend, Valerie (yes, the same Valerie who hosted the Halloween party ten months prior). The text read something like, "Hey! Stefan is back in town visiting. Would you be up to meeting soon for a drink and appetizers?"

I couldn't believe it. I hadn't heard from Stefan in nearly a year so this felt like being passed a note in the 7th grade, "My friend thinks you're cute! He wants to know if you'll go with him."

A week later I attended what would be the most hilarious and awkward first date of all time. I showed up at the restaurant, a popular local spot that is super causal and fun. At the table sat Stefan, Valerie, and…Valerie's dad! The four of us had a totally PG date that was chaperoned. What in the world have I gotten myself into now?

Stefan and I began a long-distance relationship for nearly a year. Due to the distance, we couldn't see each other very often and spoke or communicated only occasionally. I wasn't even sure if we *were* dating, because the last time I dated *Friends* was on TV and now I had no idea what the rules even were.

There were several weeks in between our first date with Valerie's dad and our next. At the second, which was really our first date but our third time meeting each other, our conversation began superficially with a quick, "what have you been up to lately?" to which I answered, "I bought a house today."

Stefan was caught off guard. "You bought a house?! *T O D A Y!?"* He laughed nervously and quipped, "who does that?! Where is this place?!" I had, indeed, closed on the house earlier that afternoon. The house was empty, but I had the key and asked if he wanted to see it.

I told him (well, warned him) I bought this home as an investment and that it was, eh, a little rough around the edges, but that I had a vision as I had planned to fix it up and sell it and live there while doing so.

When we arrived at my story-and-a-half bungalow, I'm not sure what scared him more; the roof falling off the back of the house or the gaping holes in the living room floor which made it possible to see into the basement. He sort of shyly said, "um…yeah, it's uh…nice." I don't think he had ever met a single woman who'd bought a house before; or at least not one like this.

My part-time real estate gig was blooming alongside my primary career. I adopted a rescue dog from the shelter and named him Marley. I was practicing yoga regularly.

Around this time, I received a life-changing job offer. This position was a substantial move in a leadership role and would more than triple my salary. My relationship with Stefan progressed and by Fall of 2016 he moved in, joining Marley and me in the renovations of the bungalow. Stefan and I got married in Summer 2018.

We sold the bungalow that fall and moved into a big white house on the hill, which also needed renovations, but was by all accounts a massive improvement. We were enjoying the trappings of my success. Things were going great, right?

They say with big responsibilities comes big expectations, or something like that. Yes, I was drawing an enormous salary and had a beautiful home and nice cars and took a trip to Paris. It was awesome. And fun. And rewarding. And…demanding.

The expectation had been that I would be available 24-hours a day, 7 days a week, 365 days a year. Yes, even Christmas Day. Yes, even on vacation. Because that is what I agreed to when I accepted the position.

Remember, we're not labeling things as "bad" or "good," we're just naming them, observing them. What we're attempting to do here is learn to find the balance. So, while I was enjoying this success to the fullest, I was also beginning to experience some mental and physical signs that I was overloaded and heading for burnout. And, like many of us, I was too busy to notice.

This culture, often characterized by long working hours, the relentless pursuit of productivity, and the undervaluation of leisure and rest, has significant implications for mental health. Hustle culture promotes the idea that value and self-worth are directly linked to professional achievements and productivity.

This mindset can lead to chronic stress, a condition characterized by a perpetual state of heightened physiological and emotional tension. Chronic stress is associated with a host of mental health issues, including anxiety, depression, and burnout.

Burnout, in particular, is a state of emotional, physical, and mental exhaustion caused by prolonged and excessive stress. It occurs when we feel overwhelmed, emotionally drained, and unable to meet constant demands. As the stress continues, we begin to lose interest and motivation that led them to take on a certain role in the first place.

Constant busyness has diminishing returns. While hustle culture purports that constant busyness leads to greater success, research suggests that there are diminishing returns to overwork. Prolonged working hours often lead to decreased productivity, creativity, and cognitive function.

The human brain is not designed for prolonged periods of concentration and requires rest to function optimally. Moreover, constant busyness leaves little time for activities known to bolster mental health, such as physical exercise, socializing, and engaging in hobbies. The neglect of these activities can exacerbate feelings of loneliness, anxiety, and depression.

The psychological effects of constant busyness and working tirelessly are profound and multifaceted. Fueled by societal expectations and exacerbated by social media, this leads to chronic stress, anxiety, depression, and burnout. It undermines the very productivity and success it purports to promote by neglecting the importance of rest and recovery.

As society becomes increasingly aware of these detrimental effects, there is a growing movement towards valuing work-life balance and recognizing the importance of mental health. What I hope to do here is challenge the norms of hustle culture and promote a more balanced and harmonious approach to work and life.

There are some things that show up in our lives as a result of being overworked, stressed, anxious, and burned out that you may find surprising. Perfectionism, people-pleasing, and procrastination can be patterns that show up in our lives over and over.

If I hear one more person tout these behaviors as badges of honor, I swear I am going to turn this car around so fast! But before I beat you up over this, let's dive in.

These behaviors were prominently on display in my life for many, many years, showing up in full force when I took the big corporate job because I was stuck in the maladaptive thinking pattern that these were *good* things. Isn't a *good* thing to want to do a good job? Isn't it a *good* thing to want the project to be "perfect" before releasing it to the public? Isn't a *good* thing to want to do things for other people?

And what about procrastinating? It's not your ADHD (well, it might be sometimes) as much as it is your dysregulated nervous system.

For me, especially during this time of my life, procrastination was showing up in ways I wasn't fully aware of, such as housework. I prided myself on keeping a super clean house but sometimes the laundry piles up or the bathrooms are dirty, and I just didn't care as much as I used to.

To avoid the work, I would put off my least favorite assignments until the last possible minute. I was also avoiding uncomfortable conversations, a good diet, exercise, and true, deep feelings. All signs that I was totally dysregulated. Some other common yet dismissed signs you're dysregulated include reactivity, irritability, high anxiety, avoidance (known as dorsal vagal shutdown), and even anger.

The intricate interplay between the nervous system and human behavior manifests vividly in patterns of procrastination, perfectionism, and people-pleasing. These behaviors, often considered as mere personality traits or bad habits, can actually be understood through the lens of nervous system deregulation.

Nervous system deregulation occurs when the body's autonomic nervous system (ANS) – responsible for controlling involuntary bodily functions, including stress responses – becomes imbalanced. The ANS comprises the sympathetic nervous system (SNS), which triggers the "fight-flight-freeze-fawn" response during perceived threats, and the parasympathetic nervous system (PNS), which promotes "rest-and-digest" functions, restoring the body to a state of calm.

Deregulation happens when there's excessive activation of the SNS, leading to chronic stress and anxiety, or when the PNS fails to adequately engage, preventing proper relaxation and recovery. We're going to take a deeper dive into how this works in Chapter 6, but for now let's introduce ourselves to some of the most common behavior patterns that are indicators of dysregulation.

Procrastination and Nervous System Deregulation

Procrastination, the act of delaying or postponing tasks, is often a manifestation of stress and anxiety. When you perceive a task as threatening or overwhelming, the sympathetic nervous system activates the stress response, leading to avoidance behaviors.

Procrastination can be seen as a temporary escape from the discomfort of stress, a misfired coping mechanism where the brain opts for immediate relief over long-term goals. Chronic procrastinators often experience a vicious cycle of stress, delay, and further stress, perpetuating nervous system deregulation.

Perfectionism Linked to Deregulation

Perfectionism, or the relentless striving for flawlessness, is closely linked to an overactive sympathetic nervous system. Perfectionists often set unrealistically high standards for themselves, and the fear of failing to meet these standards can trigger the SNS, leading to heightened stress and anxiety.

This constant state of alertness can keep the nervous system in a perpetual state of deregulation. Ironically, the stress and anxiety caused by this strive for perfection can impair performance, leading to procrastination and a further increase in stress, creating a self-sustaining loop of nervous system deregulation. This is why you are so tired. Your body is working very hard to keep this maladaptive system going.

People-Pleasing as a Response to Deregulation

People-pleasing behavior, the tendency to overly accommodate others to the detriment of one's own needs, can also be understood through the lens of nervous system deregulation. This behavior often stems from a heightened stress response to social disapproval or conflict.

The desire to avoid negative judgments or confrontations can activate the SNS, driving individuals to engage in people-pleasing as a form of conflict avoidance. This behavior can lead to chronic stress, as it often involves suppressing one's own needs and desires, further contributing to nervous system deregulation.

The Role of the Parasympathetic Nervous System

The PNS plays a crucial role in mitigating the effects of nervous system deregulation. Activities that engage the PNS, such as deep breathing, meditation, and yoga, can help counteract the stress response and promote relaxation. For individuals struggling with procrastination, perfectionism, and people-pleasing, practices that activate the PNS can be particularly beneficial.

These activities can help break the cycle of stress and avoidance by fostering a state of calm and reducing the physiological triggers of these behaviors. Psychological interventions, such as cognitive-behavioral therapy (CBT), ACT, and DBT, can also address the underlying anxiety and stress contributing to these behaviors.

CBT focuses on identifying and challenging distorted thought patterns and developing healthier coping mechanisms. By addressing the cognitive aspects of procrastination, perfectionism, and people-pleasing, individuals can learn to manage their stress responses more effectively, promoting nervous system regulation. ACT is a form of psychotherapy that uses mindfulness strategies to help people live and behave in ways consistent with their personal values (remember from Chapter 1) while developing psychological flexibility.

It encourages the acceptance of what is out of one's personal control and commitment to action that improves and enriches one's life. The core of ACT is to stop denying and avoiding painful experiences and instead accept these as part of life, choosing to pursue actions aligned with personal values despite the potential discomfort.

Dialectical Behavior Therapy (DBT) is a cognitive-behavioral therapy treatment method developed by Marsha M. Linehan in the late 1980s. It's primarily aimed at helping people with conditions involving emotional dysregulation by focusing on the synthesis or integration of opposites, particularly acceptance and change. This is done by teaching what is known as skills in mindfulness, emotion regulation, distress tolerance, and interpersonal effectiveness.

The correlation between nervous system deregulation and behaviors such as procrastination, perfectionism, and people-pleasing highlights the profound impact of physiological processes on psychological patterns. These behaviors are not merely personal failings or quirks but can be understood as responses to underlying stress and anxiety driven by nervous system deregulation.

By recognizing the physiological roots of these behaviors, individuals can adopt strategies to promote nervous system regulation, such as engaging the PNS through relaxation practices and seeking psychological interventions. Ultimately, addressing nervous system deregulation offers a path towards not only alleviating these maladaptive behaviors but also promoting overall well-being and resilience.

Perspectives on Mental Health and the Hustle

In 2024, my team and I conducted a survey to find out how the hustle is affecting mental health. The survey, entitled *Impact of Hustle Culture on Health*, revealed some insights that I want to share with you.

Of the results, 100% of respondents reported that they experienced **stress** due to the hustle culture, 92% reported experiencing **burnout**, and **anxiety** was reported by 78%. Mental health conditions that fell to the bottom of the pile were depression and feelings of isolation, however those numbers were still over 30%. So, what can do about this?

Radical Self-Care Tools and Resources

Combating the psychological effects of the hustle culture necessitates a holistic, integrated approach based on your specific needs at any given time. Everything from irritability, anxiety, procrastination, people-pleasing, and perfectionism requires a multifaceted approach that focuses on overall well-being.

Radical self-care involves prioritizing your needs and well-being, implementing strategies that promote psychological flexibility, and adopting tools and resources that encourage a healthier lifestyle and mindset.

Here are some practical tools and resources to help you address these issues.

1. Mindfulness and Meditation: Incorporate daily mindfulness practices, such as mindful breathing or body scans like Press Pause, to help ground yourself in the present moment, reducing the overwhelm that can lead to procrastination or perfectionist tendencies.

2. Time Management Tools: Pomodoro Technique: Use a timer to work in short sprints (25 minutes), followed by short breaks. This can help manage procrastination by breaking tasks into more manageable parts.

3. Journaling: I realize journaling isn't for everyone, but for those who do like it, here are some prompts.

Reflective Journaling: Use journaling to reflect on instances of procrastination, people-pleasing, or perfectionism. Identify triggers and emotions associated with these behaviors, and brainstorm healthier responses or solutions. This is a great place to use some curiosity. Why is this triggering? What emotions am I feeling from this trigger?

Gratitude Journaling: This can shift focus from what you perceive you need to do perfectly to appreciation for what you have and can do, which can reduce the pressure from perfectionism.

4. Therapeutic Approaches: ACT and DBT Skills: Learning and applying skills from Acceptance and Commitment Therapy (ACT) and Dialectical Behavior Therapy (DBT), such as mindfulness, acceptance, and distress tolerance, can be powerful. Look for therapists, books, or online resources that specialize in these therapies.

5. Physical Activity: Regular Exercise: Engaging in regular physical activity has been shown to improve mood, reduce anxiety, and enhance overall mental health, helping to combat the stress that often fuels procrastination, people-pleasing, and perfectionism.

Yoga and Tai Chi: These practices combine physical movement with mindfulness, promoting a balanced approach to self-care.

Implementing these tools and resources requires commitment and patience. Start small, choosing one or two strategies to integrate into your life, and gradually build on them as you become more comfortable. Remember, the goal of radical self-care is to foster a healthier, more harmonious approach to life, addressing not just the symptoms but the root causes of the psychological effects of the hustle.

Chapter 5
Mind-Body Connection
Learning to Listen to Yourself

"I've tried yoga, but I find stress less boring."

— Anonymous

I was 40 years old when, in the summer of 2018, Stefan and I got married. Due to my "advanced age" we set about the business of starting a family right away. We were healthy, vibrant people who never thought much of it, but after months of trying to conceive without success, it became clear we needed to consult a physician.

I went to my doctor and asked for some guidance. She said that I'm healthy and vibrant and sometimes it just takes time. I asked for some testing but to my surprise, she was resistant to this, saying, "by every indication, you should be able to conceive. But if you really want me to, I'll refer you to a specialist."

The specialist ordered a whole bunch of bloodwork and pelvic exams before giving me an hour-long interview asking all sorts of questions about my medical history, family history, and more. After a review of the interview and bloodwork, the specialist asked, "why are you here, again?" Um, to have a baby....

The specialist informed me that all the tests and interview questions revealed that I am....vibrant and healthy and should have no problems conceiving and to come back, "only if it takes a while." Ah, managed care.

Another year went by. And...nothing. This time I went to a specialist in another city. And, same thing. They asked if I ovulate regularly. Yep. They asked if I have a regular period. Yep. They ran more tests. Then we began a process known as IUI - Intrauterine insemination. To do this, I had to inject myself with fertility drugs to force my body to produce as many eggs as possible. Then, I went back to the doctor every time I ovulated, where they would use the IUI procedure to increase the chances of conception. After four rounds of this and no baby, I was at my wits end.

The doctor sat us down and said, "we don't know why you're not getting pregnant. Our next step is IVF. There is a 25 percent chance of pregnancy with IVF for someone your age."

To which I replied, "so there's only a 25 percent chance of us having a baby?"

The doctor said, "oh, no. There's a 25 percent chance of pregnancy. There's a far less chance that you'll actually go home with a baby."

This is when I realized the doctor and I were not working towards the same goal, and it was a crushing blow because I wish I had known this a year prior. We went home defeated and I spent the next several days on the couch feeling sorry for myself. I took time off of work, cleared my calendar, and allowed myself to feel whatever feelings were coming up.

After several days, I was ready to rejoin life. I asked myself, "what are we doing!?" This is when I used curiosity to come to a life-changing realization: Was our goal pregnancy, or was our goal to become a family? The answer was clear.

Despite what I learned in seventh grade health class and every after-school special on television, it's actually not that easy for some people to get pregnant. And, the answer to the question, *where do babies come from?* is…all sorts of places.

According to the CDC, in the United States among married women aged 15-49 with no prior births, about 1 in 5 are unable to get pregnant after one year of trying. Also, about 1 in 4 women in this group have difficulty getting pregnant or carrying a pregnancy to term. Further, the CDC notes that Functional Hypothalamic Amenorrhea (FHA) is a condition caused by excessive exercise, weight loss, stress, or often a combination of these factors.

A medically reviewed article in 2020 reported that several recent studies have found links between the woman's levels of day-to-day stress and lowered chances of pregnancy. For example, women whose saliva had high levels of alpha-amylase, an enzyme that marks stress, took 29% longer to get pregnant compared to those who had less.

This is how curiosity changes your life. I began to get out of living in the problem and began leaning into possibility by using curiosity. I made a list (yes, a literal list on a legal pad) of what *was* possible.

The list included things like: What attorneys do I know, and do they practice family law? What/where are the local foster care agencies? Who do I know who has adopted before? What are the costs/fees for adopting? Domestic or international? How long does adoption take? Suddenly, everything shifted.

We decided to pursue both private adoption and foster care simultaneously. These are two vastly different mechanisms with exceptionally different processes. For the private adoption side, we decided to 'DIY-it" instead of going through a huge agency, finding a lawyer who specialized in family law. She instructed us to make a profile book of our lives, which is like creating a profile for an online dating website, except for babies. "Here's us kayaking! Here we are at the Eiffel Tower! We are super cool people, please choose us for the baby inside your body!" We took the book to several OB-GYN offices and dropped them off. And waited.

We then contacted a foster care agency. A social worker came to our home to interview us and to begin our home study, which is a comprehensive process that adoption agencies and social workers use to evaluate prospective adoptive parents. It's an essential step in the adoption process, ensuring that a child is placed in a safe, loving, and stable home.

We happen to know a social worker who conducts home studies, so we hired her to conduct one for the private adoption. However, foster care agencies conduct their own, so we actually had two home studies. Always overachieving, even now.

Home studies include things like an application, background checks, home visits, interviews, health assessments, financial reviews, references, and a 6-week class. It felt invasive but I was happy to learn how thorough they were.

Our class began in January 2020 and ran through mid-February. We were so excited because, "2020 is going to be OUR YEAR!" And then…2020.

The whole process came to a screeching halt in mid-March. We finally became approved, or what is known as *open*, in April and started getting calls about foster placements in June. Sometimes we'd say no for various reasons, other times we'd say yes but then the child would end up getting placed elsewhere.

The summer of 2020 was, well, you know. On August 14, 2020, I was finishing up the last course towards a yoga teacher certification. It was the first in-person activity I had done since March. The training was more than a two hour drive from home so I was in a hotel over the weekend.

Out of the blue, our social worker called and said, "there's a baby boy. He was born yesterday and he's at the hospital now. This is considered a foster placement with the goal of reunification. Are you interested in fostering him?" Easiest yes of my life.

In a fury, I shoved everything I had into a bag, grabbed my yoga mat, and flew by the hotel desk shouting, "CHECKING OUT!" as I ran to my car. My husband was home painting our basement when I called. I shouted, "there's a baby! I'm on my way home! Stop what you're doing and put together that crib that's in a box in the garage!" That basement remained unfinished for another year.

When I got home, my friend Erin and I went to Target to buy essentials. You don't know how old a child placed with you will be when you're fostering, so it's impossible to truly prepare your home. I bought a car seat, basinet, some bottles, onesies, and off we went.

Arriving back in the car, the social worker called again. "He's tested positive for NAS with a score of 6. Do you still want him?"

NAS. Neonatal Abstinence Syndrome. A score of 8 requires medication and a stay in the NICU. His score was a 6. His birth mother tested positive for methamphetamine, fentanyl, and THC, which was why he was being removed from her and placed with us.

Luckily, the big corporation where I worked has us working from home, because 2020, and they said I could take "maternity" leave for 6 weeks. We dove in head-first to learn everything we could about NAS and how to navigate the foster care system.

Many states have early intervention programs to help infants with NAS as well as a host of other developmental delays. The program in our home state is called Birth-to-Three. As luck would have it, one of the physical therapists there is a fellow yoga instructor I knew and so I called to set up an evaluation.

She came to our home to examine this helpless infant and to give us some guidance on what he needs. Another yoga teacher happens to be a pediatrician who specializes in NAS; I know, it's unbelievable. I called her, too. She said, "there are three basic objectives every day: eat, sleep, console. If you do that, and have Birth-to-Three, he will thrive."

If you don't know yoga teachers who are also experts in NAS, it's a great time to use curiosity to ask questions, learn, and dive deep into solutions and possibilities. We also watched YouTube videos on NAS care, talked to social workers, and read some research. If this baby was staying with us or not, we were going to do everything he needed to have a shot at this life he'd been given.

During this time, I simultaneously experienced a wide range of emotions and feelings on any given day. Tremendous anxiety from learning to care for a newborn with special needs and profound gratitude for being able to work from home. By now my mom was in a nursing home and cognitively unaware that this baby was with us.

My dad's health wasn't great and he was terrified of COVID so he would only visit from the outside porch – remember those days? Caring for a newborn with NAS is both challenging and remarkable at the same time. We followed the "eat-sleep-console" advice.

He ate well and slept well. His main symptom was terrible tremors; his arms and legs would shake uncontrollably. His right leg would extend out straight and then pulse back up towards his hip. His tongue would tremble.

I would wrap him in a swaddle tightly, then with a blanket. I would sit on the chaise part of the couch with a bolster under my legs to keep my knees upwards towards the ceiling and hold him in the little nook between my hips and knees. But every now and then his whole body would tremor and shake, which was a constant reminder his undeveloped nervous system was trying to rid itself of the powerful drugs to which he'd been exposed. Tremors in newborns with NAS are a physical manifestation of the neurological and physiological stress associated with detoxification.

One day the social worker called to inform us that the birth mother had been granted visitation. So, on an unseasonably warm October day I took him downtown to a community services agency and handed him over to a social worker whom I'd never met. I had been taking care of this baby around the clock for the entirety of his short life and now had to hand him over to a total stranger.

The social worker was present during the entire visit, observing how the birth mother interacted with the baby. I was not allowed in the visitation. Instead, I left for the duration of the hour-long visit and went to a local coffee shop to try distracting myself from intrusive thoughts. I picked him up exactly 60 minutes later.

Since it was so warm outside, I decided to take him on the city's walking trail overlooking the Ohio River. I kept talking to him, telling him that everything was going to be okay no matter what happened. And I tried to focus on the warm sun on both our faces. I was deep inside my own mind, oscillating between intrusive thoughts and appreciating the warm weather and how gorgeous this baby's face looked as the sun fell gently across it.

Just then, my phone rang, pulling me out from my thoughts and back to the present moment with a thunderous jolt. It was a number I didn't recognize and since we had just left the visitation, I thought maybe it was something related to that.

"Hi, Joelle. This is the doctor's office. We have a patient who is pregnant and she's choosing adoption. She chose you from the book you brought us last year. Are you still interested in adopting?"

W H A T!? It took a minute to process her words. Wait, who is this? What, now? Can you repeat that, slower? I hung up with the nice lady and texted my husband in all caps: CALL ME ASAP!!!!!! A PREGNANT GIRL HAS CHOSEN US!!!!!!

A few days later, I was in a hospital waiting room when a woman came out and said my name. Feeling weak in the knees, I slowly stood. She led me down a long, meandering hallway where I felt out of my body and experienced tunnel vision like everything around me was in slow motion. We approached a small office on the right. Inside was a young, Caucasian blonde girl who was *really* pregnant, and in her hand was our profile book. Tears welled instantly in our eyes.

She asked quietly, "is everything in this book true?" I nodded. She said, "well, then, this is your baby." I sat down and we talked, she told me her story, we laughed and cried the happiest tears together.

She was due in three weeks. This meant the two babies would be ten weeks apart in age. I told her about the boy's NAS and the uncertainty of foster care. I asked if she was on drugs. She said, "no, I've never done drugs." And so began our relationship.

Sloane Alexandra was born in late October 2020 while I was in the room. It was the most magnificent moment of my life. I watched as her beautiful mother did the most courageous thing I've ever witnessed. As I held this precious newborn, she looked at Sloane with love and said, "baby girl, you're going to have a passport and that is something I could never give you." She then asked for tacos and Starbucks.

Minutes later, Stefan showed up with no less than 117 tacos and four drinks that all had whipped cream on top.

My relationship with Sloane's birth mother is one that very few people will ever understand. She is remarkable. And the love we share is the deepest love I've ever shared with another human.

For the next eight months, we were focused as new parents with two infants, navigating court, social workers, NAS recovery, a high-demand corporate job, and a pandemic. Oh, and at the same time I was also in graduate school pursuing a master's degree in mental health therapy.

On June 22, 2021, the baby boy's birth parents relinquished their rights in court, thereby making him eligible for adoption. Three days later, on June 25, 2021, we finalized Sloane's adoption. Four weeks after that, on July 27th, my mom died.

My mom was gregarious, eccentric, and hilarious. She often spoke of "when she dies" – and this was years before her diagnosis. She was clear that she didn't want a funeral – she wanted a party. More specifically, she wanted a parade through downtown complete with a marching band and firetrucks.

As we lined up the funeral procession outside the funeral home, my brother Dean said, "you know what? Let's give her a parade!" He walked down the line of cars, instructing them to roll down their windows, open their sunroofs or convertibles, and blast *Copa Cabana* by Barry Manilow. And that's exactly what everyone did. Can you imagine being in the town when a hearse drives by and dozens of cars behind it are singing *Copa Cabana* and dancing? It was just as she wanted. And it was perfect.

The Stress Response Cycle and the Mind-Body Connection

A pandemic, foster care, private adoption, high-demand corporate job, graduate school, and my mom dying sure sounds like a cocktail for another panic attack. And I was bracing for it. This time was different.

Instead of a psychological response, I had a physical one. I woke up one morning in early fall 2021 with my hip hurting so badly I could barely stand up. When I tried to walk, it was as if my body was a slinky. I looked like Kristen Wiig on *Bridesmaids* trying to leave the first-class cabin on the airplane and whining, "I can't get anywhere in three seconds!"

By now, I was getting trained in Integrated Somatic Trauma Therapy, so I knew exactly what was happening – my psoas muscle was spasming. We experience and store stress, anxiety, and trauma in our bodies (also called somatically). Physical signs you might be overwhelmed, stressed, or burning out include headache, fatigue, musculoskeletal pain, digestive issues, infertility, chronic mild illness, and more.

You know when you get sick and you think, "why *now!?* This is the worst time for me to get sick!" That is exactly why you got sick when you did. You were worn out and your immune system couldn't handle any more stress. The results from our 2024 survey showed that 93 percent of respondents listed fatigue at their number one physical complaint caused by stress; 60 percent said headache; and 53 percent listed digestive issues.

Although somatic trauma therapy and somatic healing have been around for quite some time, they've been recently popularized by social media and the creation of several apps aimed at teaching somatic healing techniques to release stored emotions and trauma in the body. It is a body-centered therapy that focuses on the connection between mind and body in the healing process. It operates on the understanding that trauma symptoms are the effects of instability of the ANS.

Through somatic techniques, such as deep breathing, grounding, and movement exercises, this therapy aims to help people release the tension, anxiety, and energy stuck in the body due to past traumatic experiences, thus restoring the ANS to a more regulated state. However, the fundamental goal of somatic therapy and healing is not to down-regulate an activated nervous system, but rather to garner awareness that your body is in a state of response.

My stress response to everything that happened in my life in 2020 and 2021 was musculoskeletal as evidenced by my hip going on the fritz. The psoas muscle that runs through the hip girdle is part of the ANS, specifically the sympathetic nervous system. It's part of our alarm system that gets activated during the stress response cycle. The psoas is the physical location in the body where the fight-flight-freeze-fawn response occurs. When our brain receives an 'alarm', our body goes into fight-flight-freeze-fawn by the psoas muscle engaging or becoming activated. Next, a chain reaction of things happens, such as our body producing glucose, cortisol, and adrenaline to prepare us for "fighting or fleeing."

Famed researcher Hans Selye coined the phrase the *Stress Response Cycle* in the 1930s. According to a 2018 article published in the Singapore Medicine Journal, Selye, who is known as the 'father of stress research', disavowed the study of specific disease signs and symptoms, unlike others before him, and instead focused on universal patient reactions to illness.

His concept of stress impacted scientific and lay communities alike, in fields as diverse as endocrinology, complementary medicine, animal breeding and social psychology. The stress response cycle has 4 stages; Alarm, Resistance, Exhaustion, and Recovery.

In stage one, the body's alarm system is sounded off by stimulus or stimuli received by one of the five senses. Stage two occurs when our brain tries to decipher if this alarm is life-threatening or non-life threatening. Stage three is a state of high-activation (e.g., fight-flight-freeze-fawn), and stage four is when the autonomic nervous system returns to a state of calm, coming out of the sympathetic response and into the rest-and-digest of the parasympathetic response.

The problem is that most of us stay in stage three – a state of activation – chronically because we lack awareness of mind-body connection and how our body is responding to emotional and mental stressors in our lives. We ignore ourselves, living in the hustle culture of 'I have to "push through" or "get through" the next project, season, issue', etc.

The cumulative effect of staying in stage three chronically is that we begin to have chronic disease like those listed above plus high-blood pressure, heart disease, infertility and even conditions like eczema. With so much at stake, why wouldn't you do anything you could to reduce the inflammation in your body and complete the stress response cycle?

Completing the stress response cycle is so easy you're going to think I'm making this up. The challenge is that you must first be aware that it's happening, and then you must begin to pay attention, on purpose, to your body, mind, and the mind-body connection.

Finally, you have to take inspired action towards processing and resolution. While the ways to complete the stress response cycle are almost infinite, there are a few that work beautifully and are easy and free.

1) Physical Activity. You knew this one was coming. If you're still complaining about exercise and movement and having all the excuses and all the "I know I should's" – listen up. *You have to move your body.* In this context, the type of movement almost doesn't matter, but walking or yoga, especially yoga with hip openers, are the top choices here.

Remember in Chapter 2 when I told you that you create your own chaos? The stories we tell ourselves and the excuses we have around movement and exercise takes the cake. Stop it. Stop the excuses and the stories about moving your body. Get up. Go for a walk.

It doesn't matter how many steps you take, how much you sweat, or what your biofeedback device is asking of you. What matters here, in the context of completing your stress response cycle, is moving your body. That is because the sympathetic response (e.g. the psoas) is engaged because it thinks you need to prepare for fighting or running, which triggers a whole host of chemical and hormonal chain reactions like the ones previously mentioned.

That is a massive amount of energy coursing through your body looking for somewhere to go. If you don't move your body to release it and return to a state of calm, your autonomic nervous system becomes overloaded, resulting in the short-term effects of headache, upset stomach, mild chronic illness (like a cold or the flu), digestive issues, sleeplessness, and irritability, along with the cumulative effects of chronic disease, heart disease, stroke, high-blood pressure, infertility, and more. Stop the story. Get up and move.

2) Get Outside. The research is clear about how spending time outdoors is beneficial to our nervous system, emotional and mental states, and physical health. A 2021 peer-reviewed study (Coventry, et al.) found that nature-based interventions, specifically gardening, green exercise, and nature-based therapy, are effective for improving mental health outcomes in adults, including those with pre-existing mental health problems. Further, the study suggests that spending 20-90 minutes outside daily for eight to twelve weeks improves overall health outcomes in nearly every category. Don't overthink it. Go sit on your porch and drink some coffee.

3) Creative Outlet/Hobbies. Remember those things you love but haven't done for a while because you "don't have time?" Doing something you love simply for the sake of it is a great way to complete the stress response cycle. It's also a fantastic way to use curiosity and pressing pause to reset the ol' nervous system. That guitar that's hanging on your wall – go play it.

Has it been a while since you played pickleball? Go grab some court time. Do you love being creative in the kitchen? Plan a gorgeous meal and spend time there this weekend with some great music and get to it! What about reading, yoga, taking an improv class, coloring, or learning to play the ukulele? Find something that brings you utter joy and do that. Often.

4) Connection. Connecting with other people as well as to yourself is paramount in restoring the body and mind to a state of calm. In the hustle culture of texting and social media messages, the art of conversation is waning. Whether it's on the phone or in-person, we need human connection. Something I started doing with my friends at the end of a nice dinner as we're hugging or after phone calls is saying we love each other. Tell people you love them. Make it weird.

When you combine a few of these things together, you are exponentially increasing your ways to complete the stress response cycle as well as return to the sympathetic state of rest. If you grab a friend and go for a walk outside, you are combining physical activity with being outside with connection to another person. This is the trifecta of perfection when it comes to completing your stress response cycle. Yes, it is that easy! The challenging part is learning to get curious enough to become acutely aware of when you need it, which in our modern society is basically every day. Then, delibarately and intentionally paying attention to your mind-body connection so you can move your body and return to a state of calm.

Your body is going to love it, your mind is going to love it, your blood pressure is going to lower, and you might even stave off some cognitive decline for several more years. Get outside. Move your body. And connect with other humans. You're going to have more capacity for whatever tomorrow brings; and you're going to be healthier, happier, and less of a jerk to be around.

Radical Self-Care Tools and Resources

The biggest, most important lesson I hope you takeaway from this book is awareness. In today's fast-paced world, cultivating awareness of the mind-body connection is crucial for maintaining physical and mental health.

Being attuned to how stress manifests in the body – such as through muscle tension, headaches, fatigue, back and shoulder pain, teeth grinding, painful periods, GI issues, eczema and more – allows you to address these symptoms before they escalate. This heightened awareness enables a proactive approach to health as you learn to listen to your body and respond to your own needs effectively.

Furthermore, understanding this connection helps you recognize the impact of mental and emotional stress on physical well-being, guiding you towards holistic practices that balances both the mind and the body. By fostering a deep understanding and awareness of yourself, you can make informed choices that will enhance your resilience and overall health, counteracting the often detrimental effects of the hustle culture.

What's an effective way to practice body awareness? The

Press Pause method. We learned this in Chapter 3, and now we're reinforcing it here to deepen the practice.

Press Pause

1. **Start by Finding a Comfortable Position:** You can lie on your back on a comfortable surface or sit in a comfortable chair. If lying down, let your legs extend out slightly apart, and rest your arms by your sides, palms facing up. If sitting, keep your back straight and your feet flat on the floor. The key element here is to make yourself as comfortable as you can. There is no "right way" to do this – only to do what feels good for you.
2. **Close Your Eyes or Soften Your Gaze Downward:** This can help reduce distractions and make it easier to focus on bodily sensations. You can use an eye pillow, towel, t-shirt, bandanna, or anything else to cover your eyes.
3. **Breathe Deeply and Relax:** Place one hand on the heart and the other on the belly. Take a long, slow, deep breath through your belly, nose, and windpipe. It's helpful to make a quiet sound while doing this, like an ocean or how you might imagine Darth Vader's breathing.
4. **Focus on Your Body:** Begin at your feet and slowly move your attention through different body parts.

Notice sensations like warmth, coolness, tension, pain, or relaxation without trying to change them.

5. **Move Up Through Your Body:** Gradually move your focus from one part of the body to the next—up through the legs, torso, arms, and head. Pay attention to each area for a few moments before moving on.
6. **Observe Without Judgment:** If you notice discomfort, tension, or other sensations, simply observe them without judgment. The goal is not to change the sensations but to become aware of and simply observe them.
7. **Use Your Breath:** Imagine breathing into and out of various parts of your body, which can help deepen your sense of relaxation and awareness.
8. **Conclude Your Practice:** After you've scanned your entire body, take a few deep breaths, move your awareness to your hearing as you slowly bring in some external sounds. When you're ready, slowly open your eyes. Take a moment to notice your overall state and how your body feels.

Chapter 6
Preparing for Obstacles

"In the middle of every difficulty lies opportunity."

— Albert Einstein

On August 13, 2021, just two weeks after my mom died, we celebrated our beautiful boy's first birthday. We named him Parker. At this point, he was still considered to be in foster care; however, he was now eligible for adoption, and we were moving toward that.

So, from June 22nd through August 13th, we were approved to adopt Parker. We finalized Sloane's adoption, my mom died, and we celebrated Parker's first birthday. We celebrated Sloane's first birthday just ten weeks later, in October. On December 3, Parker's adoption was finalized. Four years after beginning our journey towards becoming a family, we finally relaxed and celebrated—big time.

It's important to note these life events because most of us live our lives with some level of constant 'chaos' and a total lack of awareness about how these events are truly affecting us. This is not to say that these things are to be labeled as 'bad'; rather, the point is to bring awareness around how we move through our lives—completely and utterly disconnected from ourselves and totally unaware of the magnitude to which our body and mind are responding to regular daily life.

We're on autopilot. We're like zombies walking around with copious amounts of coffee, hoping our socks match while pretending to be functioning humans.

Here's the thing: things are going to happen. Curve balls are coming, whether or not we want them. Your car is going to break down, someone is going to piss you off, a loved one will get a terrible diagnosis, your electricity will go out during a storm, and someone will inevitably eat the last piece of cake that you've been dreaming about all day.

Life presents sudden challenges that can profoundly disrupt our routines and plans, and then our sense of self-care goes out the window. Whether it's a family member's sudden illness, the loss of a loved one, or other significant life changes like divorce or job loss, these events require us to navigate a new reality, one often filled with uncertainty and emotional turmoil.

Let's explore how to prepare for unexpected disruptions, ensuring that we not only cope with immediate challenges but also lay a foundation for sustained emotional and physical health.

In his book, *The Obstacle is the Way,* New York Times Best Selling author Ryan Holiday teaches us to frontload our expectations to prepare for setbacks. The idea of premortem (not to be confused with postmortem, which is investigating after the fact to 'do better next time') is meant to help us plan for when the shit hits the fan. Holiday says, "*External factors rule your world. Promises aren't kept. You don't always get what is rightfully yours, even if you earned it. Be prepared for this.*"

Curiosity is our friend here. To prepare our plan, it helps to brainstorm about the 'what ifs'. It's impossible to plan for everything that might go wrong in our lives. It can also be detrimental to think about everything that could go wrong, especially if you're a person with anxiety, panic disorder, or OCD and already live in a constant state of worst-case thinking.

What we're trying to do here instead is build a toolbox of things to help us when our world turns into a shit storm and we feel like the wind has been knocked out of us. Doing so builds resilience and emotional intelligence, and reduces the setback's length and impact.

Understanding the Impact of Unexpected Life Events

The idea to write this book started several years before I sat down and started typing. And that's true for many of us, especially for our dreams and goals. So many people "have a book in them" with beautiful and complex stories to tell. Why does it take us so long to accomplish what's in our hearts?

Because…life. We're busy doing everything to keep ourselves and others alive, which fundamentally is the purpose of this book – to give you permission to pause and create more mental capacity and bandwidth for the things that matter most to you.

My dad was a professional writer. In fact, he was an award-winning writer who was once submitted for consideration for a Pulitzer. He hated the passive voice and loved curiosity, humor, and the Oxford comma, all things I most definitely inherited from him.

A lifelong smoker and investigative journalist, he wrote a series called *Countdown to Quitting* in which he chronicled his break-up with cigarettes. He changed his diet, started exercising, and even found love late in life after meeting a lovely woman named Sharon at the gym. When Dad was 72, he and Sharon married. He was a prolific writer. Words poured out from him effortlessly. His curious mind never, ever stopped questioning everything. In 2023, when I declared that this book was finally coming to life, he promptly handed me his copy of Strunk and White, which is a must-have for any writer.

By early 2023, Dad's health wasn't great. He went into hospital in May and took his last breath on July 2. He never saw this book come together, something I will regret for the rest of my life. It is excruciating for me to write these words. While his health wasn't great, we didn't think it was the end either. Don't we always think we have more time?

Dad was interned at a national cemetery, a privilege reserved for those who have served in the U.S. military. Dad was proud of his service in the Navy during Vietnam. While he never saw combat, this is his life's single most important achievement.

He didn't want a funeral, but he was beloved by many (due to his career as a writer), and we wanted to honor him. Due to his unique sense of humor, we decided to roast him. This was two years (almost to the day) after Mom's funeral.

One of the guests who came to honor my dad was also in attendance at my mom's funeral parade. She commented, "wow, you guys really know how to throw a funeral!" I can hear my dad's signature laugh right now at the thought of "how awesome" his funeral roast was.

Unexpected life events can vary widely in nature and impact, but they typically share a common characteristic: they disrupt established routines and demand a significant emotional, physical, or financial response. The loss of a loved one, for instance, plunges us into grief, a complex emotional process that can impair our cognitive functions and physical health.

After my dad died, I developed significant GI issues, a clear sign that I was dysregulated. Remember, one of the things the vagus nerve is responsible for is digestion; pay attention to your gut, belly, acid reflux, and GI the next time you experience stress, anxiety or a setback. Similarly, a sudden illness might not only affect physical capabilities but it could also lead to significant mental health strains, influencing our mood, stress levels, and overall outlook on life.

The first step in adapting self-care routines during such times is to recognize the profound impact these events can have. Acknowledging that your feelings of confusion, sadness, or anger are valid and expected can help mitigate guilt or frustration about your disrupted routines. This acknowledgment is crucial in setting the stage for adapted self-care strategies responsive to your circumstances.

The hustle culture is not designed to handle setbacks. This is one of our biggest challenges in fighting against this long-established institution of always being connected. What happens when you have an unexpected setback, but your work didn't get the memo?

Let's take Jackie, for example, who over the weekend was doing the dishes when, suddenly, the glass she was washing broke, cutting her hand pretty badly. She tried to remain calm as she yelled for help and then off to the emergency room she went.

And there her fears were confirmed.

It was bad, so bad, in fact, that surgery was scheduled the following week to repair her hand, after which she'd be out of work for several weeks to recover.

Jackie owned her own business, and she prepared her staff in preparation for her being out for a while. She worked with her managers and clients to make sure all the proper protocols were in place for events like this. She delegated what she could to her team and notified her clients that she would be out; however, they would still be cared for by her team.

Finally, the day of surgery arrived. As Jackie waited for her turn, she lay in a hospital bed complete with the doesn't-quite-fit gown and the super fancy hospital-issued socks. She was trying to remain calm as her anxiety began to rise. The anesthesiologist arrived to discuss how the sedatives worked and what she could expect in terms of how she might feel afterward.

Just then, her phone rang. It worked. Reluctantly, she answered. The person on the other end started not with concern, care or checking on her wellbeing, but rather with, "hey, I know today is your surgery but could you just real quick answer some questions about this project?"

This is hustle culture at its finest.

This woman, who was in the hospital about to undergo surgery, was now tasked with "helping out real quick." At no point during that call did anyone ask her how she was feeling or if she was okay.

How about James? James was a top executive at a major firm. He loved his career, worked hard and took pride in his work. James was very competitive both inside and outside of the office, he was physically fit and ate well. It was well-known that if there were donuts in the canteen then don't bother asking James if wants one because he would say no!

So, you can imagine how incredibly shocking it was when James had a heart attack at his desk. He was working one day and suddenly, seemingly out of nowhere – bam. The paramedics arrived and began loading James onto the stretcher. As he attempted to gather his things, he grabbed his laptop and shoved it into his bag. He took that bag filled with work, a laptop, phone, and documents to the hospital with him. James survived and eventually returned to work.

I wish I could tell you that this story is hyperbole. I wish I could tell you that things like this don't happen. I hope you are outraged, fed up, and mad about how far the pendulum has swung in the wrong direction when it comes to expectations about work and always being available.

The survey we conducted revealed many comments from people from around the world with similar stories. One respondent commented that she was on a work call the day after giving birth to her child—the DAY AFTER GIVING BIRTH.

She returned to work after only six weeks, a common practice in the United States. Maternity leave is six months in Ireland, and more than one year in Canada. While maternity leave is planned months in advance, the way we approach work and return to work after any medical event (both planned and unplanned) needs some serious reconciling.

This is especially true if we want to retain and engage employees at every level of an organization. In this way, we can frontload the solutions to the obstacles, thereby preventing the cascading effects of colossal negative impacts on mental and physical health. When expectations are set that you must be responsive, even when dealing with a substantial or unexpected setback, the message is clear: your productivity and engagement are more valuable and important to the organization than your health.

On an individual level, we can frontload scenarios and solutions by using curiosity to answer the 'What Ifs.' *What if my kid gets sick while I'm out of town on business travel?* Think through all the possible solutions, including the exact steps you would take.

This exercise can be applied to any situation or scenario, even goal setting. Name a potential situation that would cause distress and use interest and curiosity to map out potential solutions. On an organizational level, this exercise can be applied during a leadership retreat, annual strategic planning sessions, or when developing or redeveloping human resource strategies.

"What is our plan for when an employee is out with a sudden illness, dies, unexpectedly leaves/retires, if our biggest clients left us, etc." By thinking through these problems and solutions, you are building emotional and mental resilience as well as emotional intelligence for yourself and others.

Internal Obstacles – Distractions

Not all obstacles are external. Sometimes the biggest hurdles we must overcome are our internal struggles with task initiation and focus, especially when overwhelmed, stressed out, depressed, and/or anxious. I will say something that's likely to hit a nerve or be very unpopular. Multitasking is not a thing.

Multitasking is another mechanism that the hustle culture has taught us is a 'good' thing. It's another badge of honor we proudly carry around, touting its benefits and puffing out our chests like we're holding the holy grail and can produce more in one hour than other people can all day. This is false. And here's why.

Now, before you start arguing with me in your mind like, "she's full of it. I multitask all the time! I walk with my friend every evening, and we walk and talk and sometimes drink coffee all at the same time!" That's not multitasking.

Multitasking would be more clearly defined like sending emails while participating in a meeting. A 2022 Psychology Today article written by Shonda Moralis (a Licensed Clinical Social Worker) and Sarah Dinan (a Licensed Professional Counselor), lays this out by saying that we are not multi-tasking but rather toggling back and forth between two tasks. In many cases, we would be more efficient if we single-tasked while also creating a conscious start and stop to each task.

This all starts with the cerebral cortex, the part of our brain responsible for executive processing—including thinking, planning, self-monitoring, self-control, accessing working memory, time management, and organization.

As dynamic as the cerebral cortex is, those controls are divided into two stages: goal shifting and rule activation. One stage allows us to switch from one task to another, and the other allows us to complete the task. The two cannot coexist simultaneously.

Of course, our self-identity as multitasking superhumans is tied to our sense of productivity, and our productivity is tied to our sense of self-worth. Once again, the hustle culture has taught us that not only is multitasking a thing but that it's a good thing.

In reality, your brain is physiologically incapable of this. Attempting to do this all day leaves you exhausted and run down. This then leads us back to the real culprits of distraction: The 3 Ps.

Remember the 3 Ps from Chapter 4: Perfectionism, Procrastination, and People-Pleasing. In that chapter, we discussed the 3 Ps in relation to the sympathetic response of fight-flight-freeze-fawn, so let's go a step deeper into the world of somatic therapy and somatic healing.

Stephen Porges's polyvagal theory offers a fascinating lens through which to understand the physiological underpinnings of emotional and behavioral responses, such as procrastination, perfectionism, and people-pleasing.

This theory centers on the vagus nerve, a key component of the autonomic nervous system, which influences our heart rate, digestion, and mood. It describes how different states of the vagus nerve affect our emotional and psychological resilience and reactivity.

Polyvagal Theory and Procrastination

Procrastination is often seen as a failure of self-regulation — putting off tasks despite knowing there will be negative consequences. Through the perspective of Polyvagal Theory, procrastination can be interpreted as a protective, albeit maladaptive, response of the nervous system when it perceives a threat. For someone overwhelmed by the demands of a task, the body might engage the dorsal vagal complex, leading to a shutdown state.

This state can manifest as avoidance behaviors — procrastination being a prime example. Essentially, the body is choosing to "play dead" in the face of psychological stress, similar to how a prey animal might freeze to evade a predator.

When we are 'frozen,' we can disconnect from people and things that we normally care about. Behaviors in this state can include excessive sleeping, fatigue, lethargy, and shutting people out.

Functional freeze refers to the state of being frozen; however, you're still able to function in the world, go to work, do the laundry, etc. Others may think you are engaged in the world because you're carrying out daily activities. However, in reality, you're just going through the motions of life while there is still an undercurrent of anxiety, and procrastination is high.

Perfectionism, conversely, can be linked to the sympathetic nervous system's fight or flight response, which is also modulated by the vagus nerve. A perfectionist's continual drive to meet unrealistically high standards can activate the sympathetic nervous system.

This state is akin to constantly sensing danger or a need to "fight," with the danger being failure or inadequacy in how we show up at work. The chronic stress from this constant state of alert can lead to anxiety, exhaustion, and burnout, as the body remains in a prolonged state of physiological arousal.

The Role of the Ventral Vagal System in People-Pleasing

People-pleasing, often characterized by a compulsive need to meet others' expectations at the expense of one's own needs, can be conceptualized within this theory as a survival strategy modulated by the autonomic nervous system, specifically through the actions of the vagus nerve. The distinction between different neural circuits within the vagus nerve is at the heart of Polyvagal Theory.

The ventral vagal complex controls the social engagement system and is active when we feel safe and secure. It facilitates calm states and social interaction by regulating facial expressions, vocalization, and listening. When this system is dominant, you are more likely to engage in social behaviors that promote bonding and positive interpersonal interactions, such as empathy, active listening, and nurturing behaviors.

People-pleasers often have a hyperactivated ventral vagal system in social contexts, where the drive to ensure social harmony and acceptance is strong. This can lead to behavior patterns where the person constantly monitors others' responses and adjusts their actions and reactions to avoid conflict or disapproval. While this can be adaptive in maintaining social bonds, it can become maladaptive when it suppresses genuine personal expressions and needs.

The Downside: Loss of Authentic Self

While the ventral vagal state promotes calm and connection, an overreliance on people-pleasing behaviors can lead to losing one's authentic self. The need to continuously appease others can mask true feelings and needs, leading to stress, resentment, and emotional exhaustion. This is where the adaptive function of the ventral vagal system may turn into a liability, as the suppression of authentic expressions to maintain peace can lead to internal conflict and stress.

For individuals who struggle with people-pleasing tendencies, the goal is to balance their ventral vagal activity by fostering an environment where safety does not solely depend on appeasing others. Techniques such as assertiveness training, boundary setting, and self-compassion exercises can help re-establish a sense of inner security and self-worth that is independent of external validation.

These practices encourage the expression of genuine feelings and needs, reducing the reliance on external approval for emotional well-being. Additionally, mindfulness and grounding exercises can help individuals recognize when they are slipping into people-pleasing behaviors and choose responses that are more aligned with their authentic selves. These exercises enhance self-awareness and the ability to regulate physiological responses, providing a buffer against the automatic activation of the people-pleasing response.

The Impact of Hustle Culture on the Nervous System

Hustle culture often triggers the sympathetic nervous system's fight-or-flight response. When you operate in this mode, you may appear highly productive and energetically pursue goals, but you are also at significant risk of burnout. The chronic activation of this system can lead to increased stress levels, decreased immunity, and higher susceptibility to mental health issues such as anxiety and depression.

Dorsal Vagal Withdrawal

In some cases, the persistent stress and demands of hustle culture can lead to what Polyvagal Theory describes as a dorsal vagal response. This is characterized by helplessness or defeat, where employees may "shut down" or disengage from work. This can manifest as procrastination, absenteeism, or a lack of motivation, which are often misconstrued as laziness or unprofessionalism but are, in fact, protective physiological responses to overwhelming stress.

Ventral Vagal Engagement

On the positive side, if you can foster a sense of safety and connection (ventral vagal state), you are more likely to fully engage with your colleagues and family. This state supports social engagement, creativity, and a collaborative environment. Both at work and at home, this allows for social connection and increases productivity and engagement.

Adapting Radical Self-Care Strategies for Preparing for Obstacles and Distractions

The psychological concept of RAIN, an acronym for Recognize, Allow, Investigate, and Nurture, is a mindfulness practice that can be effectively paired with Polyvagal Theory to improve emotional and mental resilience in all areas of life. It is one of the most powerful tools in our toolbox for becoming aware of one's emotional and mental state and fostering deeper self-awareness and emotional regulation.

1. **Recognize and Allow** alignment with becoming aware of your physiological state (such as figuring out if you're in fight-flight-freeze-or fawn) and accepting this state with non-judgment. This awareness is crucial for engaging in more advanced, socially engaged parts of the nervous system.

2. **Investigate** offers a direct application of understanding how our physiological responses influence our feelings and behaviors. With kindness and curiosity, you delve into understanding the causes and conditions of your emotions. What are the triggers? What sensations do you notice in your body? How do these feelings influence your thoughts and behaviors? Are you procrastinating or stuck in perfectionism or people pleasing? Investigating (using curiosity) helps you understand when you're overwhelmed so you can investigate what is triggering you in this state.
3. **Nurture** involves actively engaging the ventral vagal system, which promotes feelings of safety and connection. Tools used here include Press Pause, social interaction, or gentle exercise, which can help shift the nervous system toward a more engaged and resilient state.

How to Use All of This to Help Combat the Hustle Culture

Using RAIN and polyvagal theory can help you prepare for and respond to setbacks and the associated stress.

- **During High Stress:** Recognize the signs of stress early, allow the stress to be present without panic, investigate the triggers and body responses, and nurture oneself through the calming techniques listed above.

- **In Response to Setbacks:** Use RAIN to process feelings of disappointment or frustration. But by nurturing oneself through a setback, you can more quickly return to a state of calm and engagement, thereby giving yourself the capacity for increased productivity and more challenges.
- **Future Self:** Regular RAIN practice can enhance overall emotional resilience, psychological flexibility, and emotional intelligence, making it easier to handle future stress and setbacks. When you regularly practice techniques like RAIN, you are better equipped to maintain composure and clear thinking during times of crisis.

Chapter 7
The Right to Disconnect
Technology and the Hustle

> "Nature does not hurry, yet everything is accomplished."
>
> — Lao Tzu

For many, many years, I carried two cell phones—one for personal use and the other for work. I also managed or was responsible for several social media accounts. I worked in public relations, external affairs, and economic development, so I was part of a team responsible for managing the social media accounts of the organizations for which I worked, as well as my own personal social media accounts.

Maintaining that much energy and information is dizzying, especially when work was in crisis mode and we were 'on' all day and all night. The hustle culture tries to trick two-phoners into believing this is a good thing by purporting that having two phones creates boundaries between professional and personal lines.

In reality, having two phones requires significantly more demand on the prefrontal cortex and executive function – the areas of the brain responsible for controlling behavior and impulses, planning, decision-making, and much more. Doing so sends the prefrontal cortex offline, making the primal amygdala take over and instantly throwing you into fight-flight.

Constant stimulation of blue light from multiple sources drives down your feel-good hormones like dopamine while driving up your excitable hormones like cortisol, glucose, and adrenaline, especially when consumed first thing in the morning or right before bedtime. This is another reason why you're exhausted.

Blue Light and the Nervous System

Blue light, a short-wavelength light in the visible spectrum, has garnered significant attention due to its profound effects on the autonomic nervous system (ANS). We have already learned that the ANS is divided into two main branches: the parasympathetic nervous system (PNS) and the sympathetic nervous system (SNS).

The SNS is our activated state (fight-flight-freeze-fawn), and the PNS is our rest, calm-down state. Understanding the impact of blue light on these systems offers crucial insights into modern health challenges, particularly in an era marked by pervasive exposure to artificial light from screens and other digital devices.

Blue light exposure, especially at night, disrupts the natural circadian rhythm, which governs the sleep-wake cycle. The circadian rhythm is closely tied to the ANS and influences the balance between the PNS and SNS. The primary mechanism through which blue light affects this balance is the suppression of melatonin production.

Melatonin, a hormone secreted by the pineal gland, is crucial for promoting sleep and regulating circadian rhythms. Blue light effectively inhibits melatonin secretion, leading to delayed sleep onset and reduced sleep quality. The SNS prepares the body to respond to stress or emergencies by increasing heart rate, dilating pupils, and mobilizing energy reserves.

Blue light exposure in the evening can delay the natural decline of sympathetic activity, leading to prolonged activation of the SNS. This sustained sympathetic arousal is associated with increased heart rate and blood pressure, reduced heart rate variability, and elevated levels of stress hormones such as cortisol.

Chronic exposure to blue light, therefore, may contribute to the development of cardiovascular issues, anxiety, and other stress-related disorders by keeping the body in a prolonged state of heightened alertness. Conversely, the PNS, known as the "rest and digest" system, promotes relaxation, digestion, and recovery by slowing the heart rate, stimulating digestive processes, and conserving energy.

The suppression of melatonin and the subsequent disruption of the circadian rhythm due to blue light exposure can diminish parasympathetic activity. Reduced PNS activity at night impairs the body's ability to recover and rejuvenate, leading to poor sleep quality, impaired cognitive function, and a weakened immune response.

Over time, this imbalance can exacerbate chronic conditions such as insomnia, metabolic syndrome, and immune dysfunction. Moreover, the timing and intensity of blue light exposure play critical roles in determining its effects on the ANS. Daytime exposure to blue light, particularly from natural sunlight, can have beneficial effects by enhancing alertness, mood, and cognitive performance. It can also help regulate the circadian rhythm by reinforcing the day-night cycle, promoting healthy sleep patterns. However, exposure to artificial blue light sources, such as LED screens during the evening or at night can have deleterious effects by interfering with the body's natural preparation for sleep and recovery.

The relationship between blue light exposure and the ANS underscores the broader implications of our modern, technology-driven lifestyles on health and well-being. As digital devices become increasingly integral to daily life, understanding and mitigating the physiological impacts of artificial light is essential for maintaining optimal health.

Redefining the Workday

Traditionally, the workday had clear boundaries—starting in the morning and ending in the evening, with the physical office space as a boundary between professional and personal life. However, the rise of digital technology has fundamentally altered this dynamic. Smartphones, laptops, and cloud services mean that any space can transform into a workspace immediately.

This constant accessibility has led to the expectation that employees should be perpetually reachable and ready to engage with work matters. For many of us, this means emails are answered during family dinners, and work calls can interrupt weekends or vacations.

While digital tools have allowed for unprecedented flexibility and the ability to work from anywhere, they have also contributed to longer working hours. This shift is evident in the gradual disappearance of a clear-cut end to the workday, with many feeling the need to continue working into the night, driven by a fear of falling behind or appearing uncommitted.

Digital connectivity has changed where and when we work and the pace at which work happens. With the capability to communicate in real time, the speed of decision-making and expectations for task completion have increased. Projects that once took weeks to coordinate through back-and-forth correspondence now unfold rapidly over emails and instant messages.

This acceleration can be exhilarating and can drive significant productivity gains. However, it also raises the intensity of the work environment, compressing work cycles and leaving little time for reflection or deep thinking. Employees are required to maintain a constant state of alertness to incoming messages and updates, which can lead to cognitive overload and decision fatigue, diminishing the work's quality and the worker's health.

The ability to connect digitally at any time has cultivated a culture where constant availability is often valorized as a form of dedication to one's job. This culture is particularly pervasive in industries where competition is fierce and the margin for error or delay is minimal.

In such environments, the pressure to remain connected can lead to stress and anxiety, as the distinction between urgent and non-urgent tasks becomes muddled by the immediacy with which information is shared. Moreover, this culture of availability has significant implications for work-life balance.

Work intrusions at all hours of the day disrupt time that might otherwise be spent resting or engaging in restorative activities. Over time, this can lead to a deterioration in mental health, with increased rates of burnout, stress-related illnesses, and general dissatisfaction with one's quality of life.

Digital connectivity has also transformed traditional social interactions within and outside the workplace. Virtual meetings and teleconferences have replaced face-to-face interactions in many professional settings, affecting how relationships are built and maintained. While digital tools can facilitate communication, they often lack the nuances of in-person interactions, leading to misunderstandings and a sense of detachment.

Have you ever argued or experienced a total breakdown of an entire relationship simply because an abundance of communication was occurring over text messaging? This missed communication happens when we eliminate body language, paralanguage, and subtext by using electronic forms to "talk" back and forth. Nothing replaces time spent in person when we can look each other in the eyes, sense someone's energy, and hear their tone.

Outside of work, integrating work-related communication into personal digital spaces can erode personal relationships. The constant presence of digital devices, alerting to work issues during personal time, can prevent individuals from fully engaging with family and friends, weakening these essential support networks.

How many times have you been irritated with someone because they are on their phone while you're trying to talk with them? How many times has someone been upset with you for the same reason? The next time you're at a restaurant, notice how many people are on their phones and ignoring the person in front of them.

As digital tools have become ubiquitous, so too are many of us expected to adopt an 'always-on' mentality. Those who feel we must demonstrate our commitment and value through constant productivity and engagement often internalize this expectation. This shift has profound implications for mental health and overall well-being, as the opportunity for down-time, so critical to human health, is diminished.

While digital connectivity has brought significant benefits to the workplace, including greater flexibility and efficiency, it has also reinforced and expanded the reach of hustle culture. The challenges it poses are complex, weaving through the fabric of our daily routines and interactions. They highlight the need to critically evaluate how we engage with digital tools and manage the boundaries between work and personal life.

As we continue to navigate this connected world, understanding these dynamics becomes crucial to fostering healthier work environments and personal lives.

Global Perspectives on Work and Well-Being

Where are people getting this right, or at least not as wrong? I've been curious about this for decades. I'm a traveler, and one of the things I've noticed as I travel are the places in the world where time seems to move a little slower. It should be noted here that I once lived in New York City, and arguably, anywhere is slower than the City That Never Sleeps. Nonetheless, there are many places worldwide where people and time seem to be operating in some alternate dimension.

Let's say it's a regular Tuesday evening. You've worked eight or ten hours then rush to your kid's ballgame, after which dinner is super late and consists of whatever is easy and convenient (we'll eat healthy another day). A quick bath for the kids and get them to bed. You quickly clean up the kitchen and finally, sit down for the first time all day. You decide to fold laundry while watching your favorite show on Netflix. And then, your phone dings with that all-to-familiar sound that sends your brain into a Pavlovian state of deprivation and curiosity. You grab the phone. It's an email from work. Your primal brain kicks in, you're instantly in survival mode, and your stress hormones go into overdrive. This is the time of the day when you're supposed to unwind and reconnect with yourself, your spouse, and your vagus nerve. Instead, your stress response overloads. You are irritated, tense, and worn out. You can't fall asleep. Wash, rinse, repeat.

National Geographic Fellow and New York Times Best Selling Author, Dan Buettner, discovered the so-called Blue Zones, the places on Earth where people live the longest. Buettner has spent decades studying why some regions have more centenarians than others. The Blue Zones examine how people live in nine domains, including how we move, eat, down-regulate, and belong to a purpose and our community.

A 2023 BlueZones.com article highlights a global movement to reevaluate and modify our approach to the work week. The article outlines studies on the four-day work week, revealing intriguing outcomes. Among many other fascinating findings, the research found that for the 60+ participating companies, profits soared 35% from the prior year while resignations declined. After the pilot study, 56 companies leaned toward enacting the four-day workweek in their businesses, while two agreed to extend the trial.

School districts worldwide are also starting to investigate the four-day week, including in countries such as Poland, France, and Australia. In the U.S., nearly 900 school districts (at the time of publishing) have already moved to a four-day week.

According to the National Conference of State Legislatures, proponents of a four-day school week argue that it offers several benefits, including cost savings, improved student attendance, and increased teacher morale. By reducing the number of school days, schools can save money on transportation, food, and energy costs. Four-day school weeks can also challenge families who cannot find affordable, enriching care arrangements on the fifth weekday. Further, food-insecure students may need access to sufficient meals during the off day.

The NCSL further reported the findings of a RAND study that highlights positive qualitative findings, such as improvements in student attendance, behavioral and emotional well-being, and school climate. But it also indicates when there was no difference in quantitative data, including sleep, fatigue, and student achievement.

The point is that there is now a global movement examining different ways to approach work and lifestyle. With kids being incredibly over-programmed, is there a way to have the fifth day as a flex day where there is downtime, field trips, physical movement, time spent in nature, or learning the art of rest? These questions are meant to drive conversation around how we, as a society, can live more holistic, integrated lives that allow space for accomplishment *and* well-being.

The approach to work and well-being varies significantly across cultures and countries, reflecting diverse values and economic structures. Some countries have recognized the detrimental effects of overworking on well-being and have taken legislative steps to protect employees through systemic change.

This is a great place to pause and reflect on your own life. How often have you been on vacation, PTO, or otherwise scheduled to be off, and your boss, client, employee, co-worker, or someone else contacted or attempted to contact you? Just like Marie, who was on her honeymoon when she received a work call.

The caller said, "I know you're on your honeymoon…but…" or Linda, who was boarding a plane for a getaway weekend with girlfriends when she received not one or two but several work calls. This is the persistence and intensity of the hustle culture. And this is exactly why we need to normalize the right to disconnect.

In France, the augmentation of digital connectivity led to the legislative enactment known as the "Right to Disconnect," which occurred in 2017. This law requires companies with over 50 employees to establish hours when staff should not send or answer emails. The aim is to prevent burnout by respecting private and family time.

Germany has taken similar steps, with some companies instituting policies that limit after-hours communication. Major German companies have established guidelines that curtail the use of email after work hours to decrease employee stress and increase the distinction between work and leisure time.

Sweden is often cited for its progressive stance on work-life balance, exemplified by its experiments with six-hour workdays. Although not nationally mandated, these trials aim to increase productivity during work hours and enhance personal time after work, contributing to overall well-being.

In the U.S., the California legislature proposed a Right-To-Disconnect Law in 2024. An article by Morgan Smith published at CNBC.com in the same year shared that a proposed bill from San Francisco Assemblyman Matt Haney would make his state the first in the country to give employees the legal right to ignore non-emergency calls and emails once the workday ends. If the bill becomes law, any employer in violation could face a fine.

Countries around the world are exploring similar legislation. Italy, Canada, Australia, Luxembourg, Slovakia, The Philippines, and more are examining, piloting, and considering Right-to-Disconnect options. International approaches highlight a growing recognition of the importance of mental health and well-being in the workplace. They serve as models for how policies can be shaped to foster a healthier work environment and improve life quality, recognizing that true productivity cannot come at the expense of employee health. Through individual efforts to manage technology use and broader cultural and legislative shifts toward protecting well-being in the workplace, we can foster environments that support sustainable productivity and healthier outcomes for our overall health.

Strategies for Mindful Technology Use and Embracing a Digital Detox

Finding a balance between online engagement and real-world presence has become increasingly challenging. To counteract this, cultivating mindful technology use and periodically embracing digital detoxes can be transformative. Mindful technology use, as we understand it, involves intentionally engaging with digital tools, ensuring that these tools augment our lives without causing detriment.

This concept is crucial in managing and mitigating the pervasive effects of technology on our mental health and overall well-being. Awareness is the cornerstone of mindful technology use. Most of us engage with our digital devices on autopilot, not noticing how often we reach for our phones or lose hours scrolling through apps. To cultivate mindfulness, we must first become aware of these habits.

Once we understand our digital habits, we can set clear intentions for our technology use. This process involves aligning digital interactions with broader life goals and values. If one values focused work, they might limit social media use during office hours to foster productivity. Similarly, if family time is a priority, setting strict no-device rules during meals or family activities can help ensure that this time is quality and undisturbed.

Implementing these intentions requires specific practices. Starting and ending the day with a tech-free ritual, such as a morning jog or reading a chapter of a book at night, can help frame the day with intentionality rather than reactivity to digital stimuli. This practice sets a tone for the day, reinforcing the mindfulness we aim to maintain in our digital interactions.

Conscious digital content consumption involves choosing quality information and interactions over digital noise. This might mean subscribing to a few newsletters that provide value rather than allowing one's email inbox to overflow with unread messages.

It also means critically engaging with social media posts and news feeds, absorbing content that adds value to your life and skimming past or avoiding that which does not. Time management is another crucial element. Dedicating specific blocks of time to checking emails or social media can help prevent the day from being swallowed by unproductive digital wandering.

This practice helps maintain focus on important tasks and reduces the mental clutter that comes from constant switching between tasks. Mindfulness also extends to how we manage notifications. By customizing our devices to alert us only for the most crucial notifications, we reduce the frequency of interruptions that fracture our attention and diminish our peace of mind. This selective engagement with technology helps us maintain control over our digital interactions rather than being ruled by them.

In addition to these strategies, cultivating digital mindfulness involves developing key skills. Presence is vital, or the ability to remain fully engaged in a single task or interaction. This could mean consciously focusing on a video call without succumbing to the temptation to check emails or browse the web simultaneously.

Mindful listening and communication also play a critical role. These involve giving full attention to online interactions, ensuring digital communications are as respectful and thoughtful as face-to-face conversations. Despite the benefits of mindful technology use, challenges remain.

The addictive design of many digital platforms, coupled with societal expectations for constant availability, can make it difficult to maintain healthy boundaries. Regular digital detoxes, even if just for a day or a single evening each week, can help mitigate these challenges.

These detoxes allow us to disconnect and reset, reminding us of the world beyond our screens. Support from a community that values mindful technology use can also reinforce our efforts. Sharing strategies and experiences with others can provide new ideas and encourage adherence to mindful practices.

As our lives and technologies evolve, so too must our approaches to integrating technology in healthy, sustainable ways. Mindful technology use is not about shunning digital devices but integrating them into our lives in a way that respects our mental space and personal priorities.

By adopting and refining strategies, we can protect ourselves from the downsides of digital overload and maintain a healthier, more balanced relationship with technology. This is essential for navigating today's world without falling victim to the relentless pressures of hustle culture.

Cultivating Mindful Technology Use

1. **Set Specific Online Times.** Establish clear boundaries for when and how you use digital devices. This might mean no screens during meals, setting specific times to check emails, or turning off notifications after a certain hour. By scheduling your technology use, you can prevent your devices from dictating the pace of your day and encroaching on your personal or family time.
2. **Be Intentional With Device Use.** Before picking up your phone or logging into your computer, press pause to ask yourself why. Are you checking your email for a purpose, or out of habit? Being more intentional about your reasons for using technology can help prevent mindless scrolling and reduce the time spent on unproductive activities.

3. **Curate Your Digital Environment**. Just as you might organize your physical workspace to reduce clutter and increase efficiency, organizing your digital space can enhance focus and reduce stress. Unsubscribe from unnecessary emails, use tools to block distracting websites during work hours, and tidy your desktop regularly. A clean digital environment promotes a clean mental environment.
4. **Be Here Now.** Make a conscious effort to be present in whatever you are doing, whether working online or spending time with loved ones. When you are on your device, give your tasks your full attention. Conversely, when you are off, truly disconnect and engage fully with the world around you. This practice not only improves your concentration but also enhances your relationships and personal well-being.

Embracing Digital Detox

1. **Regularly Scheduled Detoxes:** Implement regular digital detoxes by setting aside a day or weekend where you go completely offline. Inform your contacts in advance that you will be unreachable, and plan activities that keep you engaged and relaxed without the need for digital devices. This break can help reset your relationship with technology.

2. **Vacation Detoxes:** Use vacation times as an opportunity for a longer digital detox. Vacations are ideal for disconnecting from daily routines, providing a unique chance to restore your mental and emotional health without the interference of digital noise.
3. **Mindful Morning Routines:** Start your day without digital devices. Invest in an old-school, regular alarm clock instead of using your phone as an alarm. Instead of reaching for your phone to check notifications first thing in the morning, spend the first hour of your day meditating, reading, exercising, or enjoying breakfast with your family. This sets a calm, controlled tone for the day, prioritizing personal well-being over digital demands.
4. **Technology-Free Zones:** Create spaces in your home where technology is not allowed, such as the bedroom or dining room. These areas can help foster a sense of peace and encourage non-digital activities like reading or conversing with family members.

Chapter 8
The Art of Setting Boundaries
NO is a complete sentence

"Healthy boundaries are not walls. They are gates and fences that allow you to enjoy the beauty of your own garden."

— Lydia Hall

On April 21, 2023, I turned 45. I also left the career I had spent nearly two decades building and set out to work for myself. Everyone, and I mean everyone, thought I was crazy. I constantly got questions like, "who leaves a job like that?" and "why on Earth would you walk away from a place where you had it made?" and my favorite, "you enjoy all the trappings of success! Why would you throw away that security?"

Have you thought of considering the phrase "*the trappings of success*"? It's meant to conjure visions of things we gain from success, like money, homes, cars, and vacations. When I think about that word, I think about how "trapped" I felt working in ways that didn't align with my values, had limited upward mobility, and left me exhausted.

I am not suggesting that you leave your job. In fact, quite the contrary. I am encouraging all of us to find ways to thrive while striving for greatness without burning ourselves out.

I loved my career and those I worked with, and yes, I had the trappings of financial success. However, one of the things that drove me insane, and is still my biggest pet peeve, is when someone tries to hijack my calendar.

Just because there is white space on my calendar does not mean that I am "available" during that time. When I created my business and as it continues to evolve and grow, one thing is certain: my time and my calendar are sacred. If there is space on my calendar, it does not mean I am available during that time. Maybe during that open space, I planned to meditate, press pause, go for a walk, get caught up on paperwork, drink some coffee, take a nap, call a friend, or end my day. I do everything I can so I don't have to work on certain days of the week. If someone asks if I can take a meeting then, I'll likely say no.

This is *much* easier said than done, especially when building a business. I want to be available, take meetings, and show up for clients. I also demand a more curated pace in which I have freedom and autonomy over myself and my health.

As we continue glorifying perpetual busyness and striving for success, setting boundaries becomes essential for preserving mental health and radical self-care. Hustle culture, emphasizing productivity and achievement, often blurs the lines between professional and personal life, leading to burnout, stress, and a sense of being overwhelmed.

Establishing clear boundaries is crucial in maintaining a balanced and healthy lifestyle. The importance of setting boundaries in hustle culture cannot be overstated. Boundaries are protective barriers that help us manage our time, energy, and resources effectively. They enable you to prioritize your well-being, prevent burnout, and control your life. In an environment that constantly demands more, boundaries are a form of self-respect and self-care, ensuring one's needs are not neglected in pursuing external goals. Radical self-care and mental health are intrinsically linked to setting boundaries.

Without boundaries, you are more likely to overextend, taking on too many responsibilities and neglecting your physical and emotional needs. This can lead to chronic stress, anxiety, depression, and other mental health issues. Boundaries provide a framework for identifying what is important and necessary for personal well-being, allowing you to allocate time and energy to activities that nourish and rejuvenate you.

One of the first steps in setting boundaries is identifying personal limits. This involves a deep understanding of your values, priorities, and capacities. You can revisit the values exercise earlier in this book to stay in touch with your values. Recognizing personal limits requires honest self-reflection and an awareness of how different activities and commitments impact your well-being.

It is essential to pay attention to physical, emotional, and mental signals that indicate when boundaries are being crossed, like the ones covered earlier in this book. Once personal limits are identified, the next step is effectively communicating these boundaries.

Communication is key to ensuring that others understand and respect your limits. This can be challenging, especially in environments with a culture of overwork and high expectations. However, clear and assertive communication is necessary for establishing and maintaining boundaries. It involves expressing needs and limits directly and respectfully, using "I" statements to take ownership of your feelings and avoid placing blame on others. For example, if a colleague frequently interrupts your work with non-urgent requests, you might say, "I need to focus on this project right now, but I'm happy to discuss what you need later."

This approach clearly communicates your boundaries while maintaining a respectful tone. It is also helpful to provide alternatives or solutions, such as suggesting a specific time for a discussion demonstrating flexibility and willingness to cooperate within your boundaries. Balancing professional and personal commitments without overextending yourself requires strategic planning and prioritization.

It is important to distinguish between urgent and important tasks so that time and energy can be allocated accordingly. This involves setting realistic goals and expectations for yourself and others.

Time management techniques, such as creating to-do lists, setting deadlines, and breaking tasks into manageable chunks, can help organize and prioritize commitments. One effective strategy for managing professional and personal commitments is saying "no" when necessary and then using "yes, and."

In hustle culture, saying "no" can be difficult due to the fear of missing out, disappointing others, or appearing uncommitted. However, learning to say "no" is crucial for protecting your time and energy. It is important to remember that saying "no" to additional responsibilities is saying "yes" to your well-being and priorities. This can be done politely and assertively without feeling the need to provide extensive explanations or justifications.

Another strategy is to delegate tasks when possible. Delegation lightens the workload and empowers others by giving them opportunities to take on responsibilities. This can be particularly useful in professional settings where teamwork and collaboration are encouraged.

By recognizing that you cannot do everything alone, you can create a more balanced and sustainable approach to managing commitments. Setting boundaries also involves creating designated times and spaces for work and personal activities. This helps maintain a clear separation between professional and personal life, reducing the likelihood of work encroaching on personal time.

For instance, establishing specific work hours, sticking to them, creating a dedicated workspace, and taking regular breaks, like Press Pause, can help maintain a healthier approach.

Dealing with guilt and pressure is a common challenge when setting boundaries, especially in a culture that values constant productivity. Internal and external pressures can make it difficult to uphold boundaries, leading to feelings of guilt or inadequacy.

It is important to recognize that these feelings are normal and that setting boundaries is a necessary part of self-care and maintaining mental health. One way to manage guilt and pressure is to reframe the narrative around boundaries.

Instead of viewing boundaries as limitations, they can be seen as enablers of long-term success and well-being. By setting and maintaining boundaries, you can sustain your energy and focus, ultimately leading to better performance and satisfaction in both professional and personal domains.

Self-compassion is another important tool for dealing with guilt and pressure. It involves treating yourself with kindness and understanding, acknowledging that it is okay to have limits and that taking care of yourself is not selfish. Practicing self-compassion can help alleviate feelings of guilt and foster a more positive and supportive internal dialogue.

Seeking support from others can also be beneficial in managing the pressures associated with setting boundaries. This might involve talking to a trusted friend, family member, or mentor who can provide encouragement and perspective.

In professional settings, seeking support from colleagues or supervisors who understand and respect the importance of boundaries can be helpful. Creating a supportive network can provide validation and reinforce the practice of setting and maintaining boundaries.

Mindfulness practices can also help manage the stress and anxiety associated with setting boundaries. More on this in the next chapter. Techniques such as meditation, deep breathing, and mindful self-reflection can help you stay grounded and focused, reducing the impact of external pressures. By cultivating a mindful approach, you can develop greater resilience and clarity in upholding your boundaries.

Setting boundaries in the hustle culture is essential for preserving mental health and fostering self-care. Boundaries help manage time, energy, and resources effectively, preventing burnout and maintaining control over one's life. Identifying personal limits and communicating them effectively are crucial steps in establishing boundaries.

Balancing professional and personal commitments without overextending oneself requires strategic planning, prioritization, and saying "no" when necessary. Dealing with guilt and pressure involves reframing the narrative around boundaries, practicing self-compassion, seeking support, and incorporating mindfulness.

By setting and maintaining boundaries, individuals can navigate the demands of hustle culture with greater ease, well-being, and fulfillment. The role of boundaries in radical self-care extends beyond simply managing time and energy. It also involves protecting your emotional and psychological well-being.

In hustle culture, where the focus is often on external achievements, it is easy to lose sight of internal needs and values. Boundaries serve as a reminder to honor your needs and prioritize self-care as a fundamental aspect of overall health.

Recognizing and respecting personal boundaries can also improve relationships and interactions with others. When you set clear boundaries, you communicate your needs and expectations, reducing misunderstandings and conflicts. This can lead to healthier and more respectful relationships, both in professional and personal settings. You can also encourage others to do the same by modeling boundary-setting behavior.

Effective boundary-setting requires self-awareness and a willingness to advocate for yourself. It involves regularly assessing your commitments and responsibilities, adjusting as needed.

This might mean renegotiating deadlines, delegating tasks, or stepping back from certain activities. By continuously evaluating and refining boundaries, you can ensure you align with your current needs and priorities.

Tools for Boundary Setting

1. **Evaluate Activities** and their impact on your well-being. This can help identify patterns and triggers that indicate when boundaries are being crossed. For example, if certain tasks or interactions consistently lead to feelings of stress or exhaustion, it may be necessary to set clearer boundaries around those areas.
2. **Communicating Boundaries** helps to establish your limitations in a respectful manner that will ultimately create stronger bonds and relationships. It is important to be clear and specific. Vague or ambiguous boundaries are more likely to be

misunderstood or ignored. For example, instead of saying, "I need more time," it is more effective to say, "I need an additional two days to complete this project." Being specific helps others understand the boundary and how to respect it. Using assertive language that conveys confidence and clarity is also helpful, without being aggressive or confrontational.

3. **"Yes, And".** We can build in flexibility and buffer time to accommodate unexpected events or changes. When someone asks for your help or availability during a time or season when you are slammed, busy and overwhelmed at work and home, practice using "Yes, And." If the thing they need help with isn't emergent in that moment, then try Yes, And. "Can you help me with this project on Tuesday at 4pm?" Try saying, "yes, I can help you, and how is Thursday at 10am instead?"
4. **Boundaries Aren't Just for the Office.** In personal life, setting boundaries might involve designating specific times for family, hobbies, and relaxation and protecting those times from external demands. Dealing with the guilt and pressure of setting boundaries often involves challenging internalized beliefs and societal norms.

In hustle culture, there is often a pervasive belief that more is always better, and that success is measured by constant productivity. Challenging these beliefs requires a shift in mindset, recognizing that well-being and balance are equally important measures of success. This might involve redefining personal definitions of success and finding value in rest, relaxation, and boundaries.

Chapter 9
How to Slow Down in a Hustled World

"You should sit in meditation for 20 minutes a day, unless you're too busy, then you should sit for an hour."

— Zen Proverb

Picture this: you're an over-caffeinated octopus trying to play the piano. Your eight limbs are flailing wildly, hitting all the wrong keys, and creating a cacophony that could wake the dead. That's what life can feel like without mindfulness. Imagine waking up each morning, your brain already buzzing with the day's demands before you even pee. You leap out of bed, down a gallon of coffee, and dive headfirst into a day filled with back-to-back meetings, constant notifications, and a to-do list that looks like it's plotting to take over the world. Sound familiar?

Without mindfulness, our minds become like unruly toddlers, constantly demanding attention and throwing tantrums over the smallest things. We end up reacting to life rather than living it.

It's the classic scenario: you're driving late to work, and someone cuts you off. Instead of taking a deep breath and moving on, you transform into a rage-filled maniac, shaking your hands like my Italian grandmother and inventing new swear words.

Your day spirals from there – the spilled coffee, the forgotten password, the endless stream of emails – each event piling on more stress until you're a ticking time bomb. Without mindfulness, we become masters of telling ourselves that we are multitaskers, but not in a good way. We're constantly juggling tasks, but nothing gets our full attention.

You might find yourself in a meeting, nodding along while secretly drafting an email about another project and thinking about what to cook for dinner. It's like trying to have a meaningful conversation while balancing plates on your head and riding a unicycle – something's bound to crash.

Our productivity suffers, and so does the quality of our work. We're busy, but we're not effective. Relationships also suffer when mindfulness is absent. Imagine having a conversation with a friend where you're physically present but mentally running through your grocery list.

You nod at the right times, but you're not really listening. Eventually, your friend catches on and your connections start to feel superficial. Without mindfulness, we miss the moments that make relationships rich – the shared laugh, the knowing glance, the simple joy of being fully present with another person.

Then there's the toll on our health. Chronic stress without the counterbalance of mindfulness is like leaving your car engine running in overdrive all day. Eventually, you'll run out of gas. We're more likely to experience anxiety, depression, and even physical ailments like headaches, high blood pressure, and a weakened immune system, which is the body's way of waving a white flag, begging for a break we never seem to give it.

Even sleep isn't safe from the onslaught of an unmindful life. You finally crawl into bed, exhausted, but your mind decides it's the perfect time to replay every embarrassing moment of your life, remind you of that deadline, and brainstorm a million what-ifs. Insomnia becomes your nightly companion, and you wake up more tired than before, ready to repeat the cycle of chaos.

So, what happens when we don't practice mindfulness? We become prisoners of our minds, trapped in a whirlwind of stress and distraction. We miss out on the beauty of the present moment, the depth of our relationships, and the clarity that comes from being fully aware.

Life becomes a series of frantic, disjointed episodes rather than a coherent, meaningful story. Mindfulness might not be a magic wand that fixes everything, but without it, we're like an octopus trying to play the piano – all over the place and making a mess. So, maybe it's time to put down a few of those extra arms and take a deep breath.

What is Mindfulness?

Let's start with some basics by taking a moment to understand mindfulness. What isn't mindfulness? Well, it isn't about sitting cross-legged on a mountain top, achieving enlightenment or clearing your mind of thoughts like a Jedi master, and neither is it a magical cure for turning life into a constant state of bliss – it's just being present and aware, even if that means noticing you've been daydreaming about pizza during a meeting.

Essentially, mindfulness is about paying full attention to what's happening right now in this very moment. Imagine your mind is like a spotlight, and mindfulness is about directing that spotlight to focus on the present moment rather than letting it wander into the past or the future.

It's about being completely engaged with whatever you're doing, whether eating, walking, or just breathing. When you practice mindfulness, you're like an observer of your own life. You notice your thoughts, feelings, and sensations as they come and go, but you do this without judging them.

It's like watching clouds float across the sky; you see and acknowledge them, but you don't try to push them away or hold onto them. You just let them be. This non-judgmental observation helps you see things clearly and respond to them more thoughtfully.

Another key part of mindfulness is acceptance. This means recognizing what's happening in the present moment without trying to change it. For instance, if you're feeling stressed, you acknowledge it instead of immediately trying to distract yourself or get rid of that feeling.

You say to yourself, "I'm feeling stressed right now," and let that be okay. This acceptance doesn't mean you won't act to improve things, but neither are you fighting against your current reality. To understand this better, think of a simple exercise: mindful breathing. Find a comfortable place to sit and just focus on your breath.

Notice how the air feels as it enters your nose, fills your lungs, and then leaves your body. If your mind starts to wander, it will naturally and gently bring your focus back to your breath. This process of noticing when your mind has wandered and brought it back to the present moment is the heart of mindfulness.

You can bring this mindful awareness to any activity. When you're eating, really taste your food. Notice the flavors, textures, and even the sounds of eating. When you're walking, feel your feet touching the ground, listen to the sounds around you, and notice how your body moves.

When talking with someone, give them your full attention, listen to what they're saying, and observe how you feel during the conversation. Mindfulness isn't about achieving a special state of calm or peace. It's about being present and fully engaged with whatever you're experiencing, whether pleasant, unpleasant, or neutral.

Practicing mindfulness regularly can develop a deeper awareness and appreciation for the present moment, which can help reduce stress, improve focus, and enhance your overall well-being. It's a simple but powerful way to connect more deeply with your life and world.

Mindfulness-Based Cognitive Therapy (MBCT)

Mental health therapy graduate students are encouraged to choose a theoretical orientation, which is how they will approach therapy. When I was in graduate school studying to become a therapist, I struggled to commit to a theoretical orientation because I hadn't found one that aligned with my desire to use an integrated, holistic approach to helping clients. I already had certifications in trauma-informed yoga and trauma-informed mindfulness; plus I was in my 40s, had worked in a career for more than 15 years, was divorced, and had been to therapy myself. I knew I wanted to help people with a different approach than traditional cognitive behavioral interventions.

Those interventions are fine, but I felt there must be *more.* Then, one day, I learned about MBCT and Somatic Therapy.

Mindfulness-Based Cognitive Therapy (MBCT) is a therapeutic approach that combines cognitive therapy principles with mindfulness practices. Developed by Zindel Segal, Mark Williams, and John Teasdale, MBCT is designed to help individuals who suffer from recurrent depression and other mental health conditions.

The primary goal of MBCT is to prevent the relapse of depression by encouraging a mindful approach to one's thoughts and feelings, thus breaking the cycle of negative thinking that often leads to depressive episodes.

At its core, MBCT integrates traditional cognitive behavioral strategies with mindfulness meditation techniques. Cognitive therapy focuses on changing negative thought patterns that contribute to emotional distress.

In contrast, mindfulness encourages individuals to observe their thoughts and feelings without judgment or attachment. This combination allows individuals to better understand their thought processes and develop healthier ways of responding to emotional challenges.

One of the key components of MBCT is the practice of mindfulness meditation. This involves paying close attention to the present moment, including physical sensations, thoughts, and emotions, without trying to change or avoid them.

Regular mindfulness practice teaches you to recognize and detach from negative thought patterns, reducing their impact on mood and behavior. This increased awareness helps you respond to stress and negative emotions more effectively rather than reacting automatically in ways that may perpetuate distress.

MBCT typically involves an eight-week program with weekly group sessions and daily home practice. During these sessions, participants are guided through various mindfulness exercises, such as body scan meditation, mindful breathing, and mindful movement. They also engage in cognitive exercises that explore the relationship between thoughts, feelings, and behaviors. Group discussions provide a supportive environment for sharing experiences and insights, fostering a sense of community and mutual understanding.

Studies indicate that participants who complete MBCT programs experience significant reductions in depressive symptoms and are less likely to experience future depressive episodes compared to those who receive standard care. Additionally, MBCT is beneficial for individuals with anxiety disorders, chronic pain, and other mental health conditions, highlighting its versatility and effectiveness.

One of MBCT's strengths is its focus on self-awareness and self-compassion. By cultivating a mindful attitude, individuals learn to approach their experiences with curiosity and kindness rather than criticism and judgment. This shift in perspective can lead to greater emotional resilience and a more compassionate relationship with oneself, both of which are crucial for long-term mental health and well-being.

Somatic Therapy and Somatic Healing

Somatic therapy, or body-centered therapy, is a holistic approach to healing that emphasizes the connection between the mind and the body. This therapeutic modality is grounded in the understanding that traumatic experiences and emotional distress are often stored in the body, manifesting as physical symptoms and tension.

Somatic therapy aims to release these stored traumas through body-focused techniques, promoting healing and overall well-being. The foundation of somatic therapy lies in recognizing that the body and mind are deeply interconnected. Emotional and psychological experiences are not just confined to the mind but also profoundly impact the body.

Trauma, in particular, can be stored in the body, leading to chronic pain, tension, and other physical symptoms. Somatic therapy helps individuals process and heal from emotional wounds by addressing these physical manifestations.

One of the pioneers of somatic therapy is Dr. Peter Levine, who developed Somatic Experiencing®, a therapeutic approach designed to release trauma stored in the body. Levine's work emphasizes the importance of the body's natural ability to heal from trauma, which can be supported through mindful awareness and gentle movement. Somatic Experiencing® involves helping clients become aware of physical sensations and using this awareness to release tension and trauma held in the body.

Another influential figure in somatic therapy is Pat Ogden, the founder of Sensorimotor Psychotherapy. This approach integrates somatic therapy with cognitive and emotional therapeutic techniques, providing a comprehensive framework for addressing trauma and other psychological issues. Sensorimotor Psychotherapy focuses on the body's role in regulating emotions and behaviors, using movement and body awareness to facilitate healing.

Somatic therapy encompasses a wide range of techniques to increase body awareness and release physical tension. These techniques may include breathwork, movement exercises, touch therapy, and mindfulness practices.

Breathwork involves focusing on the breath to enhance body awareness and promote relaxation. Techniques such as diaphragmatic and alternate nostril breathing can help regulate the autonomic nervous system, reducing stress and promoting a sense of calm. Movement exercises in somatic therapy often involve gentle, mindful movements that help clients become more aware of their bodies and release tension.

These movements can be as simple as stretching, or encompass more structured practices like yoga or tai chi. The goal is to help you reconnect with your body and release any physical tension associated with emotional distress. Touch therapy, another somatic therapy component, involves therapeutic touch to help clients become more aware of their bodies and release stored tension.

This can include techniques such as massage, acupressure, or other forms of bodywork. Touch therapy can be particularly effective in helping you feel grounded and connected to your body, facilitating the release of trauma, and promoting healing. Mindfulness practices are also integral to somatic therapy.

Somatic healing extends beyond the therapeutic session, emphasizing the importance of incorporating body awareness and self-care practices into daily life. This holistic approach to healing recognizes that the body and mind constantly interact and that maintaining this connection is crucial for overall well-being.

Regular exercise, healthy eating, adequate sleep, and stress management are essential to somatic healing. Exercise is particularly important in this regard, as it helps release physical tension and promotes the production of endorphins, which can improve mood and reduce stress. Activities such as yoga, tai chi, and qigong are especially beneficial, as they combine physical movement with mindful awareness, helping to strengthen the mind-body connection.

Healthy eating is another crucial component of somatic healing. A balanced diet provides the necessary nutrients for the body to function optimally and can significantly impact mental health. Foods rich in omega-3 fatty acids, antioxidants, and other essential nutrients can help reduce inflammation and support brain health, contributing to overall well-being.

Adequate sleep is also essential for somatic healing. Sleep is a critical time for the body to repair and regenerate; insufficient sleep can exacerbate physical and emotional symptoms. Establishing a regular sleep routine and creating a restful sleep environment can support the body's natural healing processes and improve overall health. Stress management is a key aspect of somatic healing, as chronic stress can have a profound impact on both the body and mind. Techniques such as mindfulness meditation, deep breathing exercises, and relaxation techniques can help manage stress and promote a sense of calm. It is also important to identify and address sources of stress in one's life, whether related to work, relationships, or other factors and to develop healthy coping strategies.

Research has shown that somatic therapy can be effective in treating conditions such as PTSD, anxiety, depression, chronic pain, and other trauma-related disorders. By addressing the physical manifestations of trauma and stress, somatic therapy helps individuals process and release emotional wounds, promoting healing and overall well-being.

One of the strengths of somatic therapy is its holistic approach. This approach recognizes that healing involves the whole person, not just the mind or body in isolation. This integrative perspective allows for a more comprehensive and effective treatment approach, addressing the root causes of distress and promoting long-term healing.

By fostering a deeper connection between the mind and body, somatic therapy helps individuals develop greater self-awareness and self-compassion, both of which are essential for overall well-being. As awareness of the importance of somatic approaches continues to grow, these therapies will undoubtedly play an increasingly vital role in mental health and wellness.

Barriers, Obstacles, and Overcoming an Overwhelming World

In the bustling chaos of modern life, practicing mindfulness can sometimes feel like trying to meditate in the middle of a rock concert. The constant noise, distractions, and demands of our hustled world present significant barriers to finding moments of calm and clarity. But don't worry; we're about to tackle these barriers head-on with practical advice.

One of the biggest barriers to mindfulness is the infamous "no-time syndrome." We're all familiar with it: our schedules are packed tighter than a sardine can, leaving little room for anything resembling stillness. We're convinced that mindfulness is a non-starter unless we can carve out an hour-long block of uninterrupted peace.

However, let's face it: waiting for an hour of uninterrupted peace is like waiting for pigs to fly. Instead, let's embrace the micro-mindfulness moments. You don't need a mountaintop retreat to practice mindfulness.

How about taking a minute of mindful breathing while waiting for your coffee to brew? Or practicing gratitude for thirty seconds while brushing your teeth? These tiny snippets of mindfulness can accumulate to make a significant difference.

Another common barrier is the expectation of a perfect meditation environment. Picture it: you, in the lotus position, surrounded by the gentle flicker of candles and the soothing sounds of a babbling brook. Now, replace that image with reality: the neighbor's dog is barking, the kids are fighting over the remote, and your phone won't stop buzzing.

The myth of needing perfect conditions can be paralyzing. But here's the truth: life is messy, and mindfulness is about finding peace amidst the mess. So, if your dog wants to join your meditation session, let him. If the kids are loud, use their laughter as a background symphony. Embrace the imperfection. Your mindfulness practice doesn't need to look like a scene from a wellness magazine to be effective.

Then there's the mind itself, a relentless chatterbox that loves to replay every embarrassing moment, fret about future disasters, and compile endless to-do lists. Attempting to quiet this internal monologue can feel like trying to herd cats. But here's a twist: instead of battling your thoughts, invite them to tea.

Acknowledge them without judgment and then gently refocus on the present moment. Picture your thoughts as clouds passing through the sky of your mind – no need to chase them, just let them float by. If your mind insists on wandering, kindly guide it back as you would a stray cat back to the path.

Consistency is another hurdle. We often set grand goals like meditating for thirty minutes daily, only to find ourselves binge-watching Netflix and wondering where all the time went. It's easy to feel like a mindfulness failure when we can't stick to our ambitious plans. But think of mindfulness as something like brushing your teeth. You don't need to scrub every corner of your mouth for an hour. A few minutes of consistent practice are enough to maintain good dental hygiene.

Similarly, short, regular mindfulness practices are more effective than occasional, intense sessions. Start with a manageable goal – even five minutes a day can be a good start – and build from there. It's about creating a habit, which is not a Herculean task.

Technology, our double-edged sword, is another formidable barrier. On one hand, we have apps and online classes that make mindfulness accessible. Conversely, our devices are often the culprits behind our fragmented attention.

Imagine you're meditating and your phone pings with a notification. Suddenly, you're torn between reaching enlightenment and finding out who liked your latest Instagram post. One solution is to use technology to your advantage by setting reminders for mindfulness breaks or using apps that guide you through short meditations.

Just remember to put your phone on *Do Not Disturb* mode – Enlightenment can wait, but that notification can wait too. Let's not forget the social aspect. Practicing mindfulness can sometimes feel like swimming upstream in a world that values productivity above all. You might even worry that taking time to meditate makes you look lazy or uncommitted. Here's a thought: wear your mindfulness practice like a badge of honor.

Share your journey with friends and colleagues, and laugh about the challenges together. Did you try meditating and end up falling asleep? Share the story! It humanizes the practice and makes it more relatable. Plus, having a mindfulness buddy can provide mutual support and accountability. It's like having a gym buddy but for your mind – someone who nudges you to practice even when you'd rather binge-watch the latest series.

Another barrier is the pesky inner critic. We often think we're not good at mindfulness or doing it wrong. But here's a little secret: there's no wrong way to practice mindfulness. It's not about achieving a Zen-like state or being free of thoughts. It's about noticing when your mind wanders and gently returning it to the present. Think of mindfulness like seasoning a stew. You might not notice the effects immediately, but over time, those little sprinkles of mindfulness add up to a richer, more flavorful life.

Celebrate the small victories, like staying present for a full minute or taking a deep breath before reacting to a stressful situation. Lastly, let's tackle the myth that mindfulness is a luxury only for those with spare time and no worries. Mindfulness isn't about escaping life's responsibilities; it's about engaging with them more fully.

It's about being present in the moments you have, whether that's while folding laundry, washing dishes, or commuting to work. You don't need to retreat to an ashram to practice mindfulness. Start where you are, with what you have. Practice mindful listening during a conversation, mindful walking during your commute, or mindful eating at lunch. These everyday moments are perfect opportunities for mindfulness.

Tools for Cultivating Mindfulness in a Hustled World

Practicing mindfulness in our hustled world requires a mix of humor, creativity, and practical strategies. By sneaking mindfulness into tiny pockets of our day, embracing the imperfections of our environment, and letting go of the need for perfection, we can cultivate a consistent mindfulness practice.

Using technology wisely, seeking social support, and celebrating small victories can also help maintain mindfulness amidst the chaos. Remember, mindfulness isn't about achieving a state of perpetual calm but about finding moments of peace amidst the chaos. So, let's put on our mindfulness capes and tackle the hustle culture one mindful breath at a time.

1. **"This Moment" Technique.** Choose a mundane task like washing your hair, brushing your teeth, or pouring a cup of coffee. It doesn't matter what you choose, just make sure it's a mundane, daily task. During the task, repeat the task to yourself for as long as you're doing it, while reminding yourself of the present moment. For example, you'd say to yourself, "the only thing that matters right now is pouring this coffee. The only thing that matters right now is pouring this coffee." Repeat as long as it takes to complete the task.

2. **Breathwork.** Yep, the simple act of breathing is an act of mindfulness practice. Using diaphragmatic breathing (breathing in through the nose and the "belly"), focus on every aspect of breathing as it occurs. Feel your ribcage expand. Notice the air moving from the bottom to the top of your windpipe. Notice your shoulders depress as you exhale. Become acutely aware of your physical body and the sensations during each moment of the breath.
3. **Mindful Eating.** Slow down when eating. Sit at a proper table. Be aware of your posture. Place your fork/spoon down between each bite. Notice everything about the food you're eating such as the texture, smell, taste, everything. Savor every bite in every moment.
4. **Mindful Listening.** There is no faster way to enhance relationships than to use active listening. Instead of listening to respond, listen to learn. What can you learn about this other person in this moment? Try to be interested rather than interest*ing*. Mindful listening requires your full attention in the moment and forces you to slow down your thinking processes.

Chapter 10
Beyond the Hustle
Rallying the World to Chill Out

"Fight for the things that you care about, but do it in a way that will lead others to join you."

— Ruth Bader Ginsburg

My kids still nap, and you would not believe the backlash we get for this philosophy and practice. And guess what? When they go down, so do we! Do we feel lazy or guilty for arriving late to family functions or missing out on something cool downtown? No! We feel rested! And our kids aren't Tasmanian devils bouncing off the walls, acting insane, or screaming because I didn't open their banana correctly. Okay, sometimes they do that but it's not because they're tired.

As we enter the final chapter of this book, I hope you've laughed and cried and maybe gained some inspiration for creating an anti-hustle lifestyle. Now it's time to put down that to-do list, kick back, and get ready for a rallying cry for a global movement of slowing down. Yes, you heard it right—

we're about to launch a worldwide campaign to "chill the hell out!"

Let's envision and create a world where people take lunch breaks, weekends are sacred, and leisure time is the new status symbol. Instead, "harmony" is the new buzzword, and our motto is "slow and steady wins the race." Now that I've shared the science and the tools with you, I'm pulling out all the stops to show you how to transform your fast-paced life into a stroll through the park. Let's be honest—hustle culture has us all wound up tighter than a squirrel on espresso.

We've turned productivity into a sport, complete with trophies for those who can juggle the most tasks while still appearing to have it all together. But now, it's time to flip the script and declare, "enough is enough!"

We're here to start a revolution where slowing down is celebrated, and radical self-care is the norm. Imagine communities where neighbors know each other's names (not just their Wi-Fi passwords)—picture workplaces where people only rush to the Friday afternoon yoga session.

Envision a world where "FOMO" is replaced by "JOMO"—the Joy of Missing Out on yet another pointless meeting that could have been an email. We're laying out the blueprint for building these serene sanctuaries. Let's share hilarious yet practical tips for turning your neighborhood from a scene out of *The Fast and the Furious* into one reminiscent of *Cheers*, where everybody knows your name and sometimes brings over a casserole.

Let's explore how companies can ditch the rat race and foster a culture that values well-being over weariness. We'll share sage advice on how to convince your hustle-addicted friends to join the movement.

From organizing "Slow Down Sundays" to creating community gardens where the only thing growing faster than the tomatoes is the sense of camaraderie, we've got a game plan that will make you want to shout, "sign me up!"

Why is the tone of this chapter so light and fun? Because we've lived in heavy and serious for far too long that it's now time to Press Pause and have fun.

One of my favorite activities is a long, slow, progressive meal. It doesn't matter if it's a midday or an evening one—as long as every seat is full, there is tons of laughter, and everyone feels a sense of belonging. This is nearly impossible to accomplish in the U.S. unless I host it at my home, which I love doing.

Restaurants in the United States have a "turn 'em and burn 'em" mentality, meaning get the customers in and out so you can make as much money as possible. Even the culture of eating is hustled. A 2017 article by AARP shared that when Americans talk about getting a coffee, they usually mean dashing into a Starbucks or Dunkin' Donuts and grabbing a takeaway latte.

When the French talk about getting a coffee, they more often than not mean actually traveling to a cafe, sitting down at a table, and sipping one that's not in a paper cup—usually with a friend. Dining is a time to relax, savor a varied diet, and talk about the day.

Americans often rush through mealtime while checking their email every few seconds.

My niece, Gillian, graduated high school in 2023. Upon graduation, she joined the Army

National Guard and will begin undergraduate school soon. I'm beyond proud of her choice to serve her country. Gillian also represents a growing trend among teens and young adults – skipping meals to be more productive.

Throughout her high school experience, she never took a lunch. That's right. The culture at her high school was such that if a student wanted to be a high achiever, to be in the accelerated and advanced classes, there was "no time for lunch." Students were permitted to eat during class, which promoted the falsity of multitasking—being able to eat, pay attention to the lecture, and take notes simultaneously.

8th grade students in the U.S. (around age 13-14) must register for the classes before beginning high school in the fall. That means we are sending a clear message to our thirteen-year-olds that productivity and achievement is more important than your health and taking midday breaks for mental and physical clarity are irrelevant. Not only this, but during a significantly important developmental period for teenagers, especially girls, we are creating negative relationships with food, mental health, and spending time in meaningful conversation with friends. What are we doing!?

Once again, I am curious about where in the world people are getting this right. Where are rates of heart disease, stroke, stress, anxiety, and depression lowest? Where are people not pushing kids into competitive sports by the age of 4? Where are teenagers taking lunch breaks?

I'm led back to Dan Buettner's work and Blue Zones. This book isn't about the Blue Zones, and I am not an expert on this topic. But it's worth noting the nine domains that have been found to be essential in building a slower pace to an intentional life and promoting substantial longevity.

By looking at the nine things in common among the areas where people live the longest and are happiest, we can develop ideas and practices that not only change us as individuals but also create community and a global movement of intentionality.

The nine things all Blue Zones have in common are: they move naturally throughout their day (working outside in their garden, walking to work, etc.); their lives have purpose (they don't just work to pay the bills); they 'downshift', or Press

Pause, a few moments every day (some do this by taking a nap, some enjoy happy hour, others meditate).

They live by the 80 percent rule (they eat until they are 80 percent full), eat loads of fruits and veggies, and drink low amounts of wine daily or weekly. They have a sense of belonging, put loved ones first (before work), and have social networks that support this lifestyle (no, hey, let's go eat the donuts in the breakroom, but rather encourage each other to thrive and live well).

Imagine a world where companies and communities are built around the idea of slowing down, spending time together, and engaging in meaningful activities rather than just working ourselves into an early grave. Picture an office where, instead of the usual Monday morning dread, people look forward to coming in because they know there's a meditation session before the day starts and a community lunch where everyone brings a dish from their cultural heritage. Sounds dreamy, right? Well, it's not just a utopian fantasy, it's entirely possible, so let's explore how we can build such communities.

Redefining the Workplace: From Hustle to Harmony

Let's start with the workplace. Imagine walking into an office that feels more like a cozy cafe than a corporate dungeon. There are comfortable sofas, green plants, and natural light pouring in. Instead of the usual buzz of stressed-out employees, you hear the soft hum of collaboration and laughter. This is where the grind has been replaced by flexible hours and a focus on mental and physical health.

1. **Morning Mindfulness and Meditation:** Kick off the day with a company-wide meditation session. Picture your boss leading a group meditation, encouraging everyone to close their eyes, breathe deeply, and let go of the stress from the morning commute. This simple practice can set a positive tone for the day and help employees feel centered and focused. And hey, who wouldn't want to hear the CEO whisper "Namaste?"
2. **Flexible Work Hours:** Companies can implement flexible work hours to accommodate different lifestyles and personal commitments. Imagine a world where you can come in later because you took your kid to school or enjoyed a leisurely breakfast with your partner. Companies show trust and respect for their team's overall life by allowing employees some flexibility.
3. **The 4-Day Work Week:** Instead of grinding away five or six days a week, let's explore the four-day work week. There's already loads of data to prove its efficacy and effectiveness. Be the trailblazer who inspires your team to try this out. Tip: The four days do not have to be Monday through Thursday, nor does

everyone have to take the same four days. Think outside the box, get creative, and be open to possibility.

Building Communities: Beyond the Office

Creating a lifestyle that prioritizes slowing down and spending time together isn't limited to the workplace. Entire neighborhoods can embrace this philosophy, turning bustling cities into havens of tranquility and connection. I invite you to come up with your own ideas or to try out some of the following:

- **Tech-Free Evenings:** Designate certain evenings of the week as tech-free. Invite family, friends, or neighbors to get together for board games, storytelling, or just talking!
- **Slow Down Sundays:** For my whole life growing up, Sundays were family days when we went to my grandparent's house, ate pasta, and hung out for hours, talking and catching up with each other's lives. Invite your family over. Put on some pasta. And hang out. Stop making this a chore and change your perspective on "if you have time, you'll swing by." Stop. Just freaking make the time. No phones allowed.
- **Come-As-You-Are Dinners:** Invite over some neighbors or friends for dinner where everyone brings

a dish to share. Everyone can explain why they chose their dish; maybe it's a family recipe with a story or meaning. Encourage storytelling where everyone can share personal stories, folktales, or something they read recently in a book. No dress code. Come here to un-win(e)d.

Leading by Example

Some companies and governments are already embracing these concepts, proving that fostering a culture of well-being and community is possible while maintaining high productivity.

Companies With a Twist: Take a look at some forward-thinking companies that have implemented policies like unlimited vacation days, mandatory "no-email" weekends, and even designated rooms for breaks and rest (not the "break room" that is a mini-kitchen with bright lights and leftover turkey sandwiches).

Try creating a workplace where it's perfectly acceptable to Press Pause to recharge your creativity. Companies which understand that well-rested, happy employees are more productive and innovative are out-pacing their competition by double-digit percentages. Follow along with Right to Disconnect legislation and encourage conversations around this topic.

Creating Cultural Shifts

For these ideas to truly take root, there needs to be a cultural shift towards valuing time spent together and slowing down. This means rethinking how we measure success and prioritizing activities that enhance our well-being. Integrating mindfulness, well-being, and community building lessons into school curriculums teaches kids about the importance of mental health and practicing mindfulness as part of their daily routine.

By teaching these values from a young age, we can foster a generation that values balance and connection over constant busyness. We can encourage companies to take corporate responsibility for the well-being of their employees seriously by offering mental health days, providing access to wellness programs, and creating a work environment that promotes breaks.

Imagine a world where corporate retreats focus on team building and relaxation rather than endless PowerPoint presentations.

Redefine Success

Remember when we talked about how you introduce yourself? Practice introducing yourself by using different languages instead of leading by what you do for a living. Redefining success in the hustle culture is like deciding to play a different game altogether. Imagine that success isn't just about who has the most impressive job title or the fattest bank account.

What if success was also measured by how many stress-free days you had this year or by how many times you remembered breathing deeply and enjoying your lunch without multitasking? It sounds revolutionary, right? Almost as if we're trading in our fast cars for comfy hammocks.

Consider the new markers of success: "I am successful because I lowered my blood pressure this year." Now, there's a goal that doesn't require a corner office or 12-hour workday. It's the success that comes from deciding to swap out your triple-shot espresso for a soothing cup of chamomile tea, and maybe even getting some extra sleep. Imagine your doctor high-fiving you at your annual check-up, not for your promotion, but for choosing to chill out more. Now, that's a success story worth telling!

Or how about this: "I am successful because this year I haven't missed one of my kids' games." Picture it: you, in the bleachers, not just physically present but genuinely engaged, cheering louder than anyone else. No conference calls during halftime, no urgent emails stealing your attention. Just you and those precious, fleeting moments that make up your child's memories. The success here isn't about how many deals you closed, it's about how often your kid looked into the stands and saw you smiling back. Now, that's a legacy.

And then there's, "I am successful because neither my husband nor I work Fridays, and that has helped rekindle our marriage with day dates and slow lunches." Gone are the days of the dreaded Friday night exhaustion, when you and your partner collapse into bed without so much as a "how was your day?" Instead, you've carved out time for a leisurely breakfast together, maybe even an afternoon bike ride followed by a round of pickleball. Your work is still getting done, but now it's balanced with the quality time that makes your relationship thrive. It's like finding the secret ingredient to a happy marriage: less grind, more grind-worthy moments together.

So, let's redefine success in a way that truly matters. Success isn't just about the accolades and the hustle; it's about the well-being we nurture, the relationships we cherish, and the joy we find in every day. Because at the end of the day, a life well-lived is the ultimate success story.

By redefining success, promoting social connections, and integrating humor and joy into our communities, we can build a culture that values well-being over constant busyness. The possibilities are endless, whether through mindful workplaces, community gardens, or themed events.

So, let's step back, slow down, and start building communities prioritizing balance, connection, and happiness. After all, life is too short to spend it all in a rush—let's savor each moment together.

Relationships Thrive When We Slow Down

Your hustle-addicted friend, let's call her Jen, is always glued to her laptop or phone, even at social gatherings. Finally, you decide it's time for an intervention, but not just any intervention—a hilariously memorable one. It all begins on a sunny Saturday afternoon.

You invite Jen over for what she thinks is a casual barbecue. Little does she know; you've orchestrated an elaborate plan. As soon as she arrives, she's greeted by the sight of you lounging in a hammock, sipping lemonade, and wearing a Hawaiian shirt that screams, "I'm here to relax, and so are you."

Jen looks confused but intrigued. "Hey, what's going on?" she asks, eyeing the inflatable palm tree in your yard.

You flash a mischievous grin. "Welcome to the Chill Zone, my friend. Today, we're going to experience the art of slowing down." Before she can protest, you hand her a lei and a pair of flip-flops.

"But I've got emails to send, deadlines to meet!" she stammers.

"Not today, Jen," you reply, leading her to a cozy setup of bean bags and a cooler stocked with refreshing drinks. "Today, we're embracing the slow life." To ease her into the idea, you start with a friendly game of Zen Jenga.

The rules are simple: each player has to take a deep breath and say something they're grateful for before pulling a block. The game proceeds hilariously slowly, with lots of laughter and mindful moments.

Next, you move on to the pièce de résistance: the Slow-Cooked BBQ Challenge. You've prepared two grills—one with instant burgers and another with slow-cooked, marinated-to-perfection ribs.

The catch? Jen has to wait for the slow-cooked ribs, which involves lounging, chatting, and no work talk. As the mouth-watering aroma fills the air, Jen begins to relax. You share stories, crack jokes, and even get her to participate in a ridiculously fun Slow-Mo Charades game where every action must be performed in exaggerated slow motion. Watching her try to mime "running a marathon" in slow-mo sends everyone into fits of laughter.

The final touch is the Digital Detox Hour. You both put your phones in a locked box and head to the backyard for hammock time. You show Jen how to sway gently in the hammock, pointing out the simple joys of listening to birds chirping and watching clouds drift by. By the end of the day, Jen is relaxed.

She bites into the tender, perfectly cooked ribs and admits, "you know, this isn't so bad. I could get used to this." And just like that, your hustle-addicted friend has taken her first step toward embracing life's slower, more intentional pace. The experience is so fun and refreshing that she's now a proud member of your new Chill Out Club, ready to spread the gospel of relaxation and balance to others.

The moral of the story? Sometimes, all it takes is some creativity, good food, and laughter to show our hustle-addicted friends that slowing down isn't just necessary—it's downright delightful.

Final Thoughts

We've dissected the beast that is the hustle culture, unraveling the glorification of relentless busyness and unmasking the toll it takes on our well-being. We've permitted ourselves to Press Pause, acknowledging that it's not only okay but also physiologically necessary.

We've laid out a roadmap for setting boundaries and provided practical tools to reclaim our time, protect our energy, and thrive while being more intentional.

Think of this book as your manifesto for a new way of living. It's a call to action for rejecting the myth that our worth is measured by how busy we are. It's about redefining success to include moments of joy, health, and genuine connection.

Let's not just dream about this world – let's build it. Let's commit to being the trailblazers who dare to slow down. Let's lead the charge in swapping burnout for harmony, stress for serenity, and perpetual busyness for purposeful living. Grab your herbal tea, put on your comfiest slippers, and let's make history—one leisurely, laughter-filled moment at a time. Join me in this radical movement to slow down, savor life, and reclaim our time.

Let's be pioneers who prove that you can thrive in your career and still make it to your kid's soccer game, that you can close the big deal and still take time for radical self-care. Together we can shift the paradigm, showing that true success includes achievement and radical self-care because life is too short to spend it all in a rush. Let's slow down, savor the journey, and show the world how it's done. It's time to start a movement that will have the world asking not "what are we doing?" but "why didn't we do this sooner?"

Where Do We Go From Here?

I know how hard it is to slow down when everyone around you is hustling. I know firsthand how impossible it seems to fight against the grain, especially when you work for a corporate giant in a demanding position or industry, are an entrepreneur, or work-from-home parent.

I've been there. I've literally sat where you're sitting, feeling overwhelmed, overrun, and exhausted. I often felt hopeless. I felt like I couldn't set boundaries with my boss or co-workers because I didn't want to appear unambitious, uncommitted, or lazy.

I felt like I couldn't set boundaries with family or friends because I wanted to show up for people when and where they asked, even if I was exhausted. But guess what – those people need those boundaries, too, even if they remain unaware of them.

The need to reevaluate the hustle is a systemic, cultural challenge that requires change. But how do we affect systemic change? By getting mad and fed up enough to demand more for your life.

I refuse to believe we must be constantly connected to achieve greatness, become the next CEO, start our own business, or any other professional goal we may have. I refuse to believe that children must be constantly programmed with year-round, insanely competitive sports and activities with zero room for boredom, creativity, or rest to 'stay out of trouble' or be successful later in life.

What are we doing? Seriously. And how can we do better?

If the mere suggestion of slowing down feels like a monumental task that is impossible to accomplish, and you had to put this book down a few times from being triggered, or you had arguments in your head with me going, "she's nuts, this will never work in my life!" then I'd say it's long overdue to do something about the pace at which you're grinding.

We will proceed by taking small, intentional steps, one at a time, slowly building up to a harmonious lifestyle. Choose one thing from this book to incorporate into your life, and choose one thing for either your work or your community.

Grab a friend and have them join you on this movement to slow down. Intentionally set time to be together and hold each other accountable for radically caring about yourselves. The whole point here is to start a conversation with your colleagues, family, friends, and anyone else you think might be feeling the same way you are. And before you say it… yes, you can.

If you're tired of being tired, it's time. If you love your job and life AND still feel exhausted, it's time. If you have changed jobs and still feel this way, the problem isn't the job – it's your relationship to the hustle, which means it's time. You get one very short, precious life. Don't waste it on things that suck the life out of you.

Let's redefine success with achievement AND radical self-care. Take one small action. And don't wait. Do it today…and bring a friend with you. This is how we move forward and answer the question, "where do we go from here?"

Deepest Gratitude for These People

I Wrote the Words. They Did Everything Else.

To everyone I've ever worked with in my "other career" – for your willingness to continue to work with me as I stepped out against the grain. I love you all so very much; it's the hustle that I don't.

To Melissa G Wilson at Networlding Publishing for seeing my vision and believing in it from our first conversation. Every meeting with you left me feeling capable and possible.

To Colin Egglesfield for introducing me to Melissa Wilson and for your unending positivity and support. Your willingness to connect people with each other and to draw their greatness out of them is your superpower. I'm forever grateful.

To Kenny Porter who once said, "you're a writer. You should write. A lot." Thank you for seeing in me what I could not see in myself and for pointing it out, just like you've done about everything for the last 30 years, even when I didn't want to hear it.

To Jean-Ann Renshaw for saying, "HELL YES!" Before I even asked the question. You are my people.

To Laura Smith for writing your book first then helping me with this one. You're the best adopted marathon runner I've ever met.

To Karen Wissing for being my go-to from day one. Thank you for always being a sounding board and for sharing your incredible gifts with me.

To Heather Ryan, Ashley Jividen, Kylie Hohman, Megan Lucas, Oksana Thomas, Tyler Kilbane, Sydney Kilbane, and Heather Sexton for welcoming me into the world of therapy and making me feel like I belong there.

To BNI Excel chapter, Wheeling, West Virginia, USA for believing in and supporting my dreams. Your unwavering support and friendship is worth more than words can describe.

To my incredible friends Amanda Dailey, Erin Carenbauer, Amy Dobkin, Shelly Carenbauer, Carah Blount, Missy Ashmore, Crissy Clutter, Nancy Haynes, Wendy Anderson, Hope Fahey, Heather Taylor, Debbie Stanton (and many others!), who go along with all my crazy ideas; and let me work on this book instead of taking the advice in it to press pause and spend time with you during the process. I realize how many topics included are things I need to improve for myself. Thank you for loving me anyway.

To my dad, Fred Connors, by whom everything I've ever written, except for this book, had been read. I'm sure you're in Heaven with your red pen, getting pissed off about all the places where passive voice is still used in this book, including this sentence.

To my siblings Dean Connors (Susan Regrut), Scott Connors (Deni Moore), and their incredible kids (who are now almost all adults) for continually encouraging me to write this and for being my biggest cheerleaders. To Dr. Alexa Connors, Kaylee Connors, Gillian Connors, Sophia Connors, and Adam Connors, thank you for contributing to this book and to my life. You'll never know how much I love you.

To my husband, Stefan. Without you this book would have taken several more years to write. Thank you for taking care of Parker and Sloane and grocery shopping and laundry and everything else while I wrote words. And thank you for listening to every word of it as I wrote it. Thank you for doing life with me. Now, let's go kayaking and chill.

About the Author

After nearly two decades in the corporate world, Joelle Moray experienced firsthand the impacts of the hustle culture on her mental and physical health. She changed her career to become a mental health therapist to help those who are stressed, anxious, depressed, and overwhelmed by the demands of modern life. Joelle Moray is a National Certified Counselor (NCC) and Provisionally Licensed Counselor (at the time of the first print of this book) in private practice.

She is the Founder and CEO of Integrate Wellness, a company passionate about disrupting the hustle culture and helping people manage their stress and burnout at work. She holds a dual master's degree in Clinical Rehabilitation and Clinical Mental Health Counseling from West Virginia University. Joelle is certified and/or trained in Integrative Somatic Trauma Therapy, Dialectical Behavioral Therapy, Acceptance and Commitment Therapy, I-CBT, Trauma-Informed Yoga, and Trauma-Informed Mindfulness. Her areas of expertise include somatic therapy, stress, anxiety, trauma, life transitions, and more.

Joelle lives in West Virginia with her husband, Stefan, and

their children Parker and Sloane, dogs Marley and Phoebe, and a cat named Norman.

To book Joelle for speaking or Workplace Wellness workshops, contact: joelle@joellemoray.com

Notes and References in Order of Appearance

Introduction

Kezic, S., Nunez, R., Babić, Ž., Hallmann, S., Havmose, M. S., Johansen, J. D., John, S. M., Macan, M., Symanzik, C., Uter, W., Weinert, P., Turk, R., Macan, J., & van der Molen, H. F. (2022). *Occupational Exposure of Hairdressers to Airborne Hazardous Chemicals: A Scoping Review.* International journal of environmental research and public health, 19(7), 4176.https://doi.org/10.3390/ijerph19074176

Islam, F., Shohag, S., Akhter, S., Islam, M. R., Sultana, S., Mitra, S., Chandran, D., Khandaker, M. U., Ashraf, G. M., Idris, A. M., Emran, T. B., & Cavalu, S. (2022). *Exposure of metal toxicity in Alzheimer's disease: An extensive review.* Frontiers in pharmacology, 13, 903099. https://doi.org/10.3389/fphar.2022.903099

Chapter 1

Madonna of the Trail. (February 19, 2024). Wikipedia. https://en.wikipedia.org/wiki/Madonna_of_the_Trail

Brewer, J. (2021). *Unwinding anxiety: New science shows how to break the cycles of worry and fear to heal your mind.* New York: Avery, an imprint of Penguin Random House.

Chapter 2

Medicine: Americanitis. (April 27, 1925). Time Magazine. https://time.com/archive/6653529/medicine-americanitis

Waytz, A. (2023). *Beware a Culture of Busyness.* Harvard Business Review. https://hbr.org/2023/03/beware-a-culture-of-busyness

Chapter 3

Bui, T., Zackula, R., Dugan, K., & Ablah, E. (2021). Workplace Stress and

Productivity: A Cross-Sectional Study. Kansas journal of medicine, 14, 42–45. https://doi.org/10.17161/kjm.

Institute of Medicine (US) Committee on Sleep Medicine and Research. Sleep Disorders and Sleep Deprivation: An Unmet Public Health Problem. Colten HR, Altevogt BM, editors. Washington (DC): National Academies Press (US); 2006. PMID: 20669438.

Chapter 5

Nazario, B. (February 20, 2020). *How Stress Can Hurt Your Chances of Having a Baby.* https://www.webmd.com/baby/features/infertility-stress

Tan, S. Y., & Yip, A. (2018). Hans Selye (1907-1982): Founder of the stress theory. Singapore medical journal, 59(4), 170–171. https://doi.org/10.11622/smedj.2018043

Coventry, P. A., Brown, J. E., Pervin, J., Brabyn, S., Pateman, R., Breedvelt, J., Gilbody, S., Stancliffe, R., McEachan, R., & White, P. L. (2021). Nature-based outdoor activities for mental and physical health: Systematic review and meta-analysis. *SSM - population health*, *16*, 100934. https://doi.org/10.1016/j.ssmph.2021.100934

Chapter 6

Holiday, R. (2014). *The Obstacle is the Way.* New York: The Penguin Group.

Moralis, S. and Dinan, S. (February 27, 2022). *The Myth of Multitasking: Why multitasking doesn't work and three ways to increase productivity.* Psychology Today. https://www.psychologytoday.com/us/blog/the-therapeutic-perspective/202202/the-myth-multitasking

Chapter 7

Blue Zones. https://www.bluezones.com/

De Felicis, J. (2023). *Four-Day Workweeks Make People Happier, More Productive, Study Shows.* https://www.bluezones.com/2023/04/four-day-workweeks-make-people-happier-more-productive-study-shows/

BBC. (December 31, 2016). *French workers get 'right to disconnect' from emails out of hours.* https://www.bbc.com/news/world-europe-38479439

National Conference of State Legislatures. (June 28, 2023). *Four-Day School*

Week Overview. https://www.ncsl.org/education/four-day-school-week-overview

Smith, M. (April 11, 2024). *Your boss could be fined $100 for bothering you after work under a newly proposed law.* https://www.msn.com/en-us/money/markets/your-boss-could-be-fined-100-for-bothering-you-after-work-under-a-newly-proposed-california-law/ar-BB1ltfwg

Chapter 9

Mindfulness Based Cognitive Therapy. (July 20, 2022) https://www.psychologytoday.com/us/therapy-types/mindfulness-based-cognitive-therapy

Somatic Experiencing. https://www.somaticexperiencing.com/somatic-experiencing

Chapter 10

AARP. (March 6, 2017). *Why the French Live Longer.* https://www.aarp.org/health/healthy-living/info-2017/french-health-longevity-weight.html